Faith & Play™

Copyright © 2008, 2010, 2012, 2017 by Faith & Play Group

QuakerPress of FGC
1216 Arch St, Suite 2B
Philadelphia, PA 19107

www.fgcquaker.org
www.QuakerBooks.org

All rights reserved. No part of this publication may be reproduced, stored in a retrieval system, or transmitted, in any form or by any means, electronic, mechanical, photocopying, recording, or otherwise, without the written prior permission of the author.

Design and layout: David Botwinik, 2 Dorset Mews, London N3 2BN, UK

ISBN 978-0-9993823-2-5 (paperback)
ISBN 978-0-9993823-3-2 (digital)

This publication was made possible by a generous grant from Obadiah Brown's Benevolent Fund

To order more copies of this publication or other Quaker titles call
1-800-966-4556 or on the world wide web at www.QuakerBooks.org

Contents

Introduction   iv

Stories of Quaker Faith and Practice   1
   Listening for God   3
   Images of God   7
   Prayer and Friends Meeting for Worship   21
   Friends Meeting for Business   28
   Gifts   33
   Queries   41

Stories about the Testimonies   51
   Love's Way   53
   Living the Ways of the Spirit   57
   Let Your Life Speak   61

Stories of Witness   67
   George Fox's Big Discovery   69
   Margaret Fell of Swarthmoor Hall   74
   Mary Fisher Carries the Quaker Message Near and Far   81
   John Woolman, Gentle Abolitionist   86
   John Woolman Visits the Indians at Wyalusing   94
   Elizabeth Fry and the Women of Newgate Prison   102

Other Stories for Friends   107
   An Easter Story for Friends   109

Appendices   115
   Resources for the Faith & Play™ Teacher   117
   A Story Session Outline for Friends   119
   Getting Started with a Circle   123
   Thoughts on Story Materials for Faith & Play™ and Godly Play®   125
   Instructions and Templates for Materials   128

Introduction to Second Edition of Faith & Play™

It is with pleasure and a deep sense of collaboration that we offer to Friends, and friends of Friends, this revised and expanded edition of *Faith & Play™: Quaker Stories for Friends Trained in the Godly Play® Method*. Stories published before 2015 have been revised based on experience and feedback, and new stories have been added along with additional supplementary materials developed to support storytellers.

Faith & Play™ is a story-based curriculum focused on building spiritual community with children and offering them images and language to express their wonder and experience of the Divine. Faith & Play™ grew out of Friends' work with the Godly Play® story curriculum, which embodies the Montessori belief that play is children's work and has dignity. These curricula support continuing revelation; multiple perspectives on a story; silence, reflection, and corporate sharing as valuable components of the spiritual life; and the diversity of ways the Spirit works within each person. While the Godly Play stories used by Friends are based on the Bible, Faith & Play stories include Quaker faith, practice and witness, as well as some Bible content told in ways that reflect Quaker sensibilities. Faith & Play stories are meant to be used in conjunction with Godly Play and we do not recommend using either resource without adequate training. See *Resources* section for more information about training opportunities for Friends.

> In his May 2008 blessing for the first Faith & Play™ publication, Godly Play® founder The Reverend Dr. Jerome W. Berryman wrote:
>
> *"The invitation to say a word of encouragement about Faith & Play™ is very gratifying. You have worked hard to understand the principles of Godly Play® and to practice the art with grace.*
>
> *The collaboration that has produced Faith & Play™ shows that you have also been mindful of children as well as the great tradition of Friends. Godly Play® seems to go where it goes, like light. If it is of God, then who knows . . .*
>
> *Blessings, laughter, deep quiet, and light . . ."*

The seeds for Faith & Play™ were planted in May 2005 when Friends attended a core Godly Play® training hosted by Philadelphia Yearly Meeting. We eagerly engaged with this method of telling Bible stories, and immediately saw the possibilities for sharing Quakerism using this method. Since "liturgy" means "the work of the people," we realized there were stories of Quaker faith, practice, testimonies, and witness to be told. We gathered as a group later that summer to begin creating Faith & Play™ stories.

Over the course of the following years, Faith & Play™ has been on a Spirit-filled journey in which the people involved have been a blessing to the work and to one another. The Faith & Play™ Group — writers, artists, storytellers, and teachers who develop the stories and materials — has welcomed new members and released others from faithful service. We were graced with the support of both Friends General Conference and Philadelphia Yearly Meeting, and throughout the development of Faith & Play™ we have been in relationship with the Godly Play® Foundation (see sidebar).

Faith & Play™ stories create a space to build spiritual community with children, offer them images and language to express their wonder and experience of the Divine, and grow in our understanding of what it means to be a Friend. This approach is grounded in a deep respect for the spiritual lives of children and the belief that play is children's work and has dignity. The Godly Play® method has resonated with Friends because it supports continuing revelation; multiple perspectives on a story; silence, reflection, and corporate sharing as valuable components of the spiritual life; and the diversity of ways the Spirit works within each person. While Godly Play® and Faith & Play™ stories are written primarily for use with children in religious education classes, they may also be experienced in the home, Friends schools, multigenerational settings, and adult religious education classes.

We did not know at the start of the Faith & Play™ journey that it would include hundreds of Friends across more than a dozen yearly meetings in the United States as well as Latin America, Africa, New Zealand, and Europe. The circle of Faith & Play™ practitioners also includes more than 20 Friends schools in the United States where the stories support the Quaker life and worshipping community of the school. We are delighted to be in relationship with the Friends World Committee for Consultation and Friends Council on Education, who support sharing Faith & Play™ in the world family of Friends and among friends of Friends.

As ever, we hope that experiences with Faith & Play™ stories will reveal new truths to each listener, and be opportunities to gather, listen, wonder, play, and put faith into practice.

In friendship and with joy,

The Faith & Play™ Group

Melinda Wenner Bradley *Candace Shattuck*
Margo Lehman *David Wakeley*
Melissa McCourt *Sallie Welte*

Faith & Play™ stories are meant to be used in conjunction with Godly Play® and we do not recommend using either resource without adequate training. See "Resources for the Faith & Play™ Teacher" section for more information about training opportunities for Friends.

Please be careful about how you use the terms "Godly Play®" and "Faith & Play™":

- Godly Play® is a registered trademark and refers specifically to the curriculum developed by Jerome Berryman.
- Faith & Play™ refers to Quaker stories developed, tested and approved by the Faith & Play™ Group.
- *Should you be inspired to experiment with this method and create and tell stories of your own, please be mindful that while they may be in the style of Godly Play® and Faith & Play™, neither label should be applied to them.*

Stories of Quaker Faith and Practice

Listening for God

A story about different ways we sense God's presence

Photo taken from perspective of the listeners.

Materials

- A 54" strip of midnight blue, charcoal, or black felt about 12" wide with a ribbon or strip of wood every 9" to indicate segments. (These colors are suggested to affirm that we experience the Spirit not only in the light but in the darkness.)
- A circle of red felt about 4" in diameter.
- Eight wooden people figures with a red dot or oval painted on each. (Use the same kind of figures that you use in the *Prayer and Friends Meeting for Worship* story.)
- A beautiful crystal, stone or other visually attractive natural object.
- A small conch shell or other natural object associated with the sense of hearing.
- A cinnamon stick or other natural object associated with the sense of smell.
- A small wooden or papier-maché dish of salt. (Salt can be stored in the basket of story materials in a small vial when not in use.)
- A feather or other natural object associated with the sense of touch.
- A miniature desert box, representing Godly Play® sacred stories. (Store sand in a sealed container in the story basket.)
- A miniature gold box representing the Godly Play® parable boxes.
- Other options for the fourth square: a miniature book, scroll, musical instrument or note to represent poetry, prayer, and song. A small cross to represent Jesus' life.

REMINDER: All story materials used should be non-toxic and non-perishable so that they can remain in the classroom at all times and be available for children's work time.

Faith & Play™ | Listening for God

WORDS	MOVEMENTS
[*Optional*: Watch where I go to get this story so you will always know where to find it. It's not where the sacred stories are. It's not where the parables are.]	*Get story materials from the Quaker story area and return to your place in the circle. Put story materials beside you.*
This is a Quaker story about listening for God and some of the different ways we sense God's presence.	
God is never far away. God's Spirit is always so close — closer than breath. But unless we stop and listen, we might not notice.	*Take out rolled up dark underlay. At "close," make this motion: with each hand cupped, palms facing and about 15" apart, one above the other, gently move hands together.*
We practice listening. We listen with our whole selves—with our bodies, our minds, our hearts, our imaginations, our souls.	*Roll out underlay from right to left about 9". Pause, looking at the new black/blue/purple space.*
Sometimes God touches us in that deep, deep place we call the heart, a place where God is at home in us and where we are at home in God.	*Place one wooden people figure on underlay. Indicate the red dot.*
We feel the Spirit's presence there. Then the Spirit helps us to know how to love, what to do, and who to be.	*Cup one hand a few inches above the figure as a sign of blessing, or of God's presence.*
We practice listening. We listen with our whole selves.	*Roll out another 9" of underlay. Pause, looking at the new space.*
Sometimes God touches us through another person. God in one person sees God in another person. Heart touches heart. This might be in friendship, love, or even when we disagree.	*Place two wooden people figures on underlay.* *At "heart touches heart," slowly move one finger back and forth several times from red dot to red dot. Then cup one hand over the figures in a sign of blessing.*
We feel the Spirit's presence. Then the Spirit helps us to know how to love, what to do, and who to be.	
We practice listening. We listen with our whole selves.	*Roll out another 9" of underlay. Pause, looking at the new space.*
Sometimes God touches us through the gifts of creation. God touches our eyes,	*Pick up stone or other small natural object and hold it up before your eyes, then place it on underlay.*

our ears,	*Pick up conch shell and bring it to your ear, then place it on underlay.*
our noses,	*Pick up cinnamon stick and pass it under your nose, then place it on underlay.*
our tongues,	*Slowly pour out a small dish of salt and move it toward your mouth, then place on the underlay.*
or our skin.	*Pick up feather and slowly pass it over the top of the opposite hand or arm, then place it on underlay.*
We feel the Spirit's presence. Then the Spirit helps us to know how to love, what to do, and who to be.	*Cup hand over objects in this panel.*
We practice listening. We listen with our whole selves.	*Roll out another 9" of underlay. Pause, looking at the new space.*
Sometimes God touches us through sacred story. God in our hearts works together with the words of the stories and we feel the Spirit's presence.	
These are the ancient stories of the people who came close to God in the desert.	*Place miniature desert box on the underlay. Slowly pour sand into the box.*
They are the story of Jesus and his parables, which are gifts to us.	*Place miniature parable box on underlay. You may add a small cross if you like.*
They may be the stories of God's people of any time or place who lived in faith and love and holy obedience.	*Book, scroll, musical note or instrument may be placed on underlay here.*
And the Spirit can come to us in other words, too, as in poetry and prayer and song.	
We welcome God in these stories and words. Then the Spirit helps us to know how to love, what to do, and who to be.	*Cup hand over objects in this panel.*
We practice listening. We listen with our whole selves.	*Roll out another 9" of underlay. Pause, looking at the new space.*
Sometimes God touches us through the community gathered for worship or for service. God touches hearts. Hearts touch hearts. The Spirit helps us to see God in each other. God is present in a special way.	*Place five people figures on underlay in a circle. Gently drop red or orange disk in the center of the circle. Cup both hands over or around the circle of figures.*

We say, "Here we are, God. Yes, we will be your people." Then we become the presence of God in the world. We become God's eyes and ears and mouth and hands and feet.

Wherever we are, we practice listening, and God can come to us in many different ways.

Unroll remaining underlay.

We listen with our whole selves—with our bodies, our minds, our hearts, our imaginations, and our souls—and God's Spirit helps us to know how to love, what to do, and who to be.

Pass hand over the entire story display from right to left.

Pause. When you begin the wondering, look up at participants to indicate you welcome their responses.

I wonder what part of this story you like best.

I wonder what part seems the most important to you right now.

I wonder if there is any part of the story we could leave out and still have all of the story we need.

I wonder if there are other ways you have felt God's presence.

You may want to indicate the open panel at the end of the underlay space.

I wonder what helps you to listen for God.

I wonder what you wonder about this story.

Images of God

A story about different ways Friends describe God

Photo taken from perspective of the listeners.

Materials

- ○ Tray or plain, wooden box to hold story (like a parable, these images are metaphors and may not "open" for you).
- ○ Black, dark charcoal or deepest blue felt underlay, 24" circle.

Faith & Play™ | Images of God

- One circular piece with flame in center.
- Six "triangular" panels with the following images: water, breath, heart, compass, simple human figure, and an open piece without an image.

Templates for the images, circle, and triangular panels, with complete instructions for creating them, are included after the story.

WORDS	**MOVEMENTS**
[*Optional:* Watch where I go to get this story so you will always know where to find it. It's not where the sacred stories are. It's not where the parables are.]	*Get story materials from the Quaker story area and return to your place in the circle. Put story materials beside you.*
This is a Quaker story about some of the ways Friends describe God's image or presence.	
God comes to each of us in different ways at different times.	
You may have images of your own. Or maybe you are not sure you have an image of God at all, or even need one. Sometimes God is simply an unseen presence.	
God is all around us, and in us. We listen deeply with our whole selves to know the Divine. There is mystery in the things we know are there but cannot see.	*Take out underlay and smooth out.*
One of the ways Friends experience God is as **Light**.	*Take flame piece from box and hold in your hands for those in the circle to see.*
Light that helps us see truths inside us.	
Light that warms us and the world around us.	
A source of energy that is always there for us.	
An Inner Light that shows the way, a guide inside us.	*Place in the center of underlay.*
A fire that burns with truth.	
God can be LIKE the Light that illuminates what we know is true inside.	*Lay hand on flame in blessing, or affirmation. Leave some space here for listeners to wonder about this.*
Sometimes Friends think of God as like **breath** or **air**. Like God, breath can be invisible to our eyes.	*Take "breath" piece from box and hold in your hands for those in the circle to see.*

8   Faith & Play™ | Images of God

In many languages, the name of God is the same word used for air or breath. [Optional: In Latin, it is *spiritus*. In Hebrew, *ruach*. The Greek word for breath, *pneuma*, also means spirit or soul.]	*Trace the "air" with your finger. Place on underlay (see photo).*
God can be like this, too.	*Lay hand on piece in blessing, or affirmation.*
Another way Friends describe God is like **water**.	*Take water piece from box and hold in your hands for those in the circle to see. Touch the water drops with your finger.*
A clear spring of pure water.	
A running river or ocean waves.	
Or perhaps a deep well that never runs dry.	*Place on underlay.*
Water that is life-giving.	
Water that satisfies our thirst and without which we cannot live.	
God can be like this, too.	*Lay hand on piece in blessing, or affirmation.*
Sometimes we say that God is **love**.	*Take heart piece from box and hold in both your hands for those in the circle to see.*
Love without end. Love without conditions. Love that connects us to one another and to all of creation. Love that heals and makes forgiveness possible.	*Place on underlay.*
God can be like this, too.	*Lay hand on piece in blessing, or affirmation.*
Sometimes Friends see God as an inner guide, like a **compass**.	*Take compass piece from box and hold in both your hands for those in the circle to see.*
A compass that helps us find our path, and helps us stay on course. A compass that always points true north so we can always find our way.	*Indicate "north" on the image.* *Place image on underlay.*
God can be like this, too.	*Lay hand on piece in blessing, or affirmation.*
There are also many images that picture God as a **person**. These are images that come close for some people.	*Take person figure piece from box and hold in both your hands for those in the circle to see.*
God is like ...	*Place image on underlay.*
The most loving **parent** imaginable.	
A **shepherd** who watches over sheep.	
A **builder** who can create something from nothing.	
God can be like this, too.	*Lay hand on piece in blessing, or affirmation.*

Faith & Play™ | Images of God

God is like these images and so many more. There are more images of God than we could ever count. All of them help us to know some part of God.

Indicate images on underlay, and spaces in between.

I do not know what might go here for you.

Place "open" image on underlay.

Trace the outline of the "open" piece with your finger.

Pause for reflection.

It may change many times during your life, and that's okay.

God is all around us, and in us. We listen deeply and with our whole selves. We use our minds, our hearts, our imaginations. In the mystery of what we cannot see we can still know God's presence in so many ways.

Indicate whole of story.

Pause. When you begin the wondering, look up at participants to indicate you welcome their responses.

I wonder what part of the story you like best.

I wonder what felt most important to you in this story today.

I wonder how some of these images of God feel for you.

I wonder what might go here for you.

Indicate "open" piece.

I wonder what other images of God you have.

I wonder where you have seen God.

I wonder if you would like to hold one of the images.

Note to storytellers:

While this is a Quaker story about some of the ways Friends imagine or know God's image, the overall artwork and design attempts to acknowledge and include key religious images from the three Abrahamic faiths. The "triangular" shapes represent the Holy Trinity in Christianity. The six triangles together form a Star of David. The pattern on the border around the triangles creates an image reminiscent of an Islamic mandala. The flame is in the center of the design to acknowledge the primacy of Light to Friends faith and religious practice.

Sources

Birchard, Bruce, "Exploring New Images of God"; *Friends Journal*, June/July 2014, Philadelphia, PA.

Kushner, Lawrence and Karen, *What Does God Look Like?*, SkyLight Paths Publishing, Nashville, TN, 2001.

Peterson, Katherine and Peterson, John, *Images of God*, Clarion Books (a Houghton Mifflin imprint), New York, NY, 1998.

Sasso, Sandy Eisenberg, *What is God's Name?*, SkyLight Paths Publishing, Nashville, TN, 1999.

Instructions for Making "Images of God"

Materials you will need:

1. One yard of felt in the color of deepest blue, black, or dark charcoal (36" x 44").
2. Large sheet (22" x 28") inexpensive black poster board. Usually available at art supply or craft stores. (Royal Brite is one such company that sells this item.)
3. One yard of patterned fabric in a shade of orange; this will be the border or "frame" that the felt pieces of the story are placed upon. (One yard is more than needed, but leaves extra if necessary.) **A few notes about purchasing this fabric:** When choosing a pattern, keep in mind that most of the pattern will be hidden under the smaller felt "triangle." Choose a geometric pattern that is not too small or busy. The pattern in photo at the end of these instructions is neither too small or too busy.
4. Small 9" x 12" felt rectangles in the following colors: cream, 4 different shades of pink and red, 2 different shades of blue, toffee brown, orange, yellow, and one piece of stiff white felt for the compass.
5. Spray adhesive, scissors and an extra fine tip Sharpie.

Step by Step Instructions:

1. Cut the yard of felt into two pieces: 18" x 44" for the smaller triangular sections and 24" x 44" for the 24" diameter circular underlay.
2. Construct a simple compass using a piece of non-stretchable string such as jute. Tie a marker or pen to one end. Measure 12" from the pen and cut the string. Anchor the end of the string with one or two fingers and draw the circle with the other hand.
3. Cut the circle out and set aside.
4. Cut the patterned fabric to 24" x 30" (2" larger than the poster board) and iron to remove any creases or wrinkles.
5. Carefully spray the poster board evenly with the adhesive. Do the same on the fabric taking care not to over saturate.
6. Carefully apply the fabric to the poster board and smooth out the fabric with your hand. Allow this to dry for a few minutes.

7. Photocopy or print out the templates. (If printing from a digital file, make sure to choose "actual size" in print set-up in order to ensure the templates are the correct size. Do not choose "fit to print." **You will need to enlarge the large triangular template by 125% and print out on 11" x 17" paper.**)

8. Cut out the large triangular template on the black line.

9. Use the large template to draw six triangles on the fabric you just adhered to the poster board. (Be consistent in how you orient the triangles on the fabric. When the triangles are cut out the pattern on the fabric should be oriented in the same manner on each triangle. See pictures provided for further detail.)

10. Using a compass, draw a 6¾" circle on the fabric adhered to the poster board. Alternatively, cut out the large circle template and use that to draw your circle on the fabric.

11. Cut out the circle and the 6 triangles. (Make sure you cut to the inside of the line you drew on the fabric so no pen or pencil marks remain when you finish cutting.)

12. Cut out the smaller triangular template.

13. Use this smaller template to draw six triangles on the felt.

14. Using a compass, draw a 5½" circle on the felt. Alternatively, cut out the small circle template and use that to draw your circle on the felt.

15. Cut out the circle and the six smaller triangles.

16. Adhere the smaller felt circle in the center of the larger fabric circle. Adhere the smaller felt triangles in the center of the larger fabric triangle-shaped pieces. The smaller felt triangle is "framed" by the fabric covered triangle pieces which create a border. As mentioned in the story teller notes, once all six triangles are put together, the border or frame should be reminiscent of both an Islamic mandala inspired by Islamic art and a Jewish Star of David.

17. Using the templates provided, cut out the images for the flame, water, heart, breath, person on the appropriately colored felt. Use the stiff white felt for the compass. **A few notes about this step:** (a) Use an extra fine tip Sharpie to draw the detail on the compass. (b) If you carefully cut out the rings for the water image, you should be able to nest all three pieces inside one another. You can also just stack the oval shapes on top of each other.

18. Mount the images in the center of the triangles and the circle using the spray adhesive.

A note about adhesives: Other adhesives like white glue can be used, but they are very wet, and are not recommended for adhering the fabric to the poster board. White glue can be used to adhere felt to felt, but be careful not to over saturate. As my art teacher used to say, "Just a dot, not a lot." Spray adhesive is "dry" but requires ventilation. Also, be sure to spray on a surface like a scrap of cardboard or newspaper to keep your work area clean.

Friend, if you have any questions about making these materials, please be in touch with the Faith & Play Group at faithandplaystories@gmail.com.

Sample Fabric

Close up photos of two triangles

Notice how the pattern on both triangular pieces is oriented in the same manner or direction.

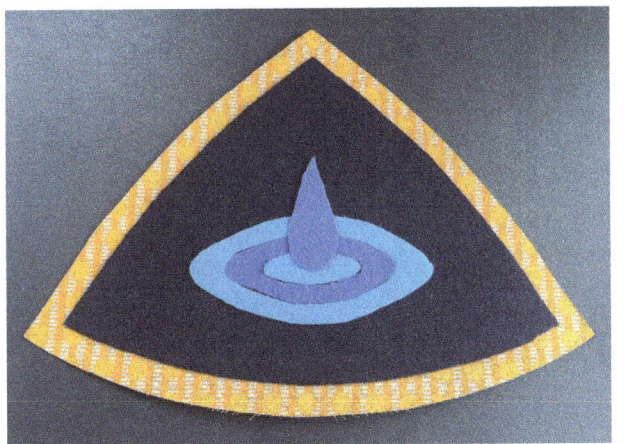

Faith & Play™ | Images of God

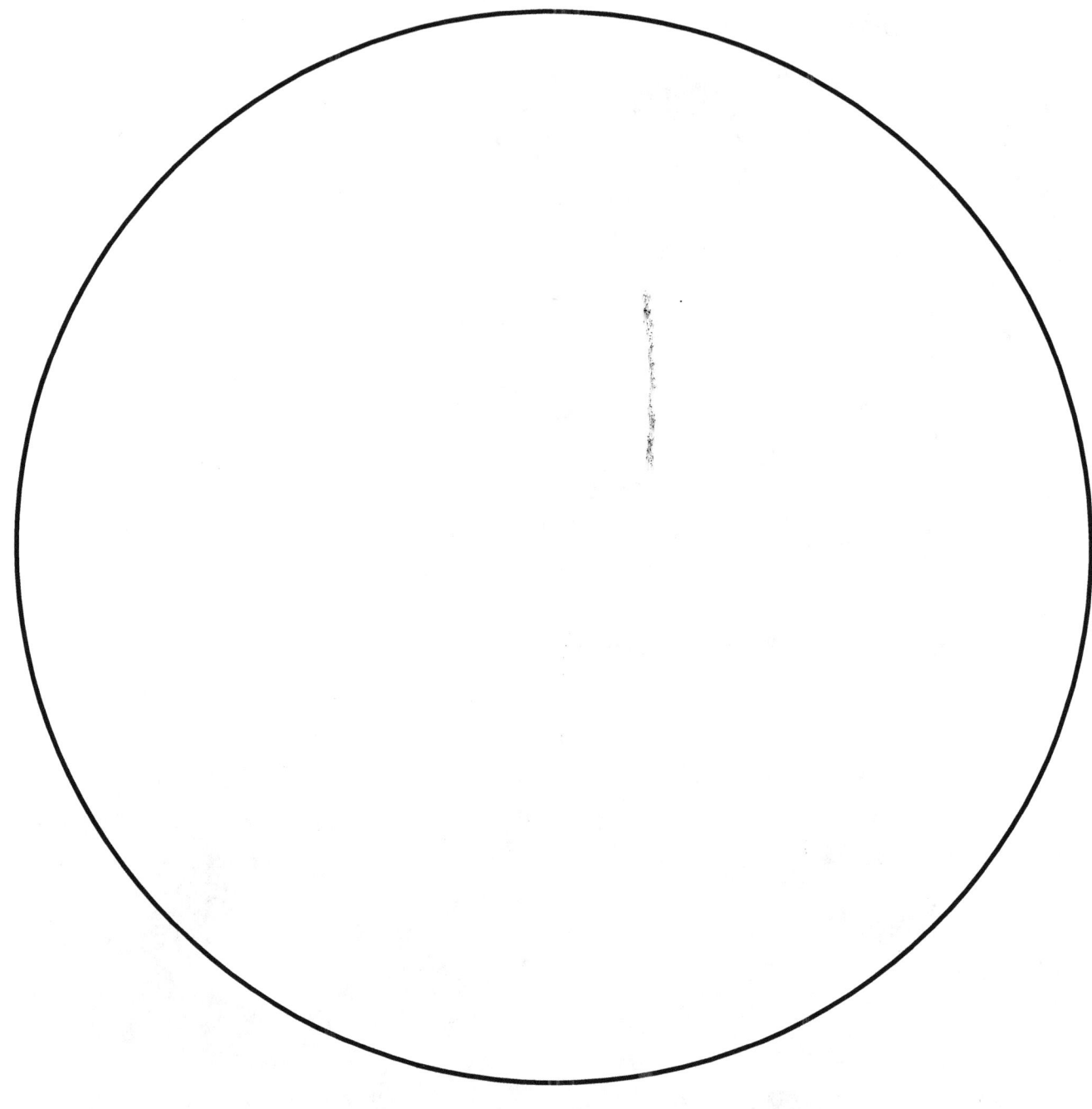

6¾" Circle

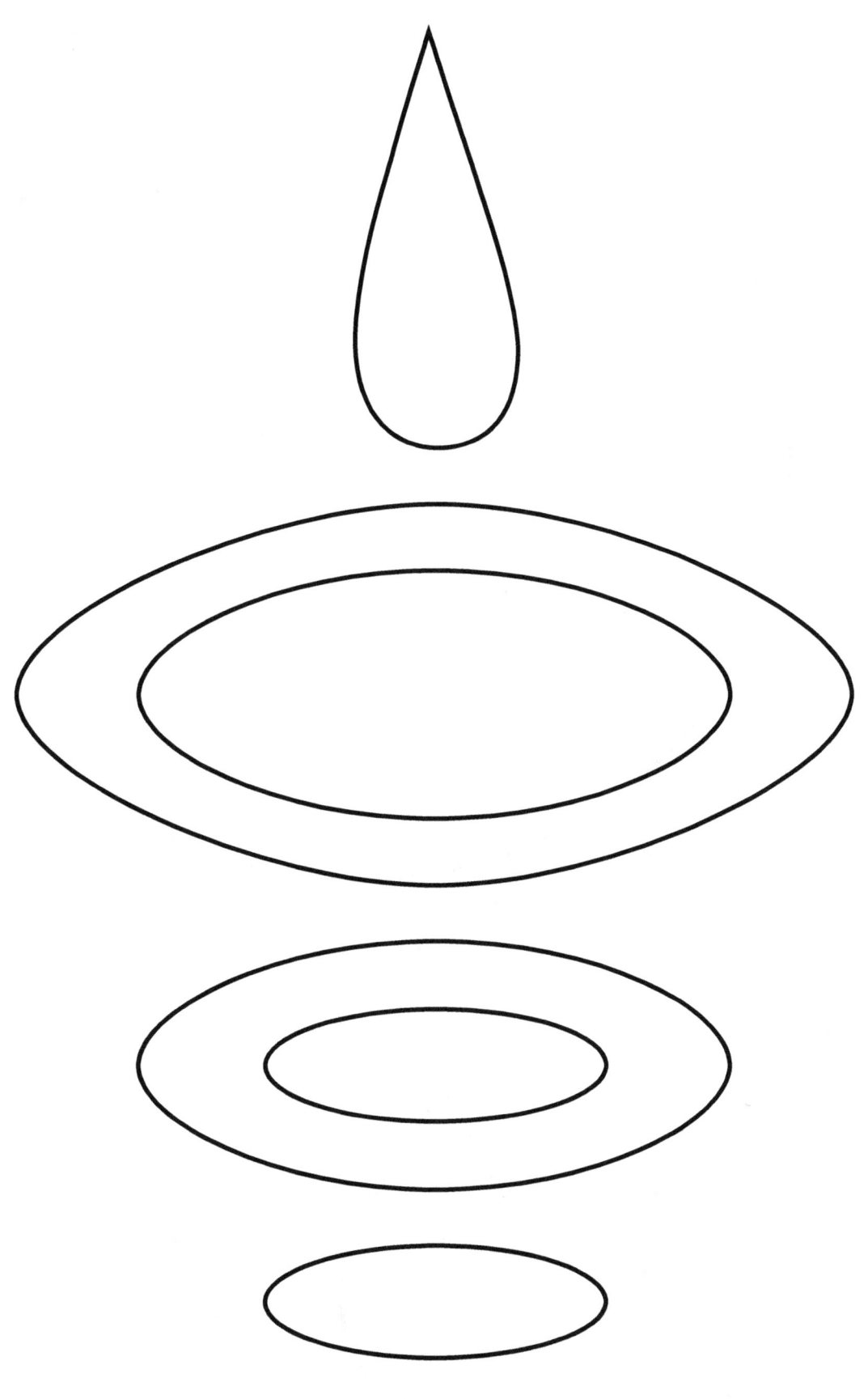

Water Template

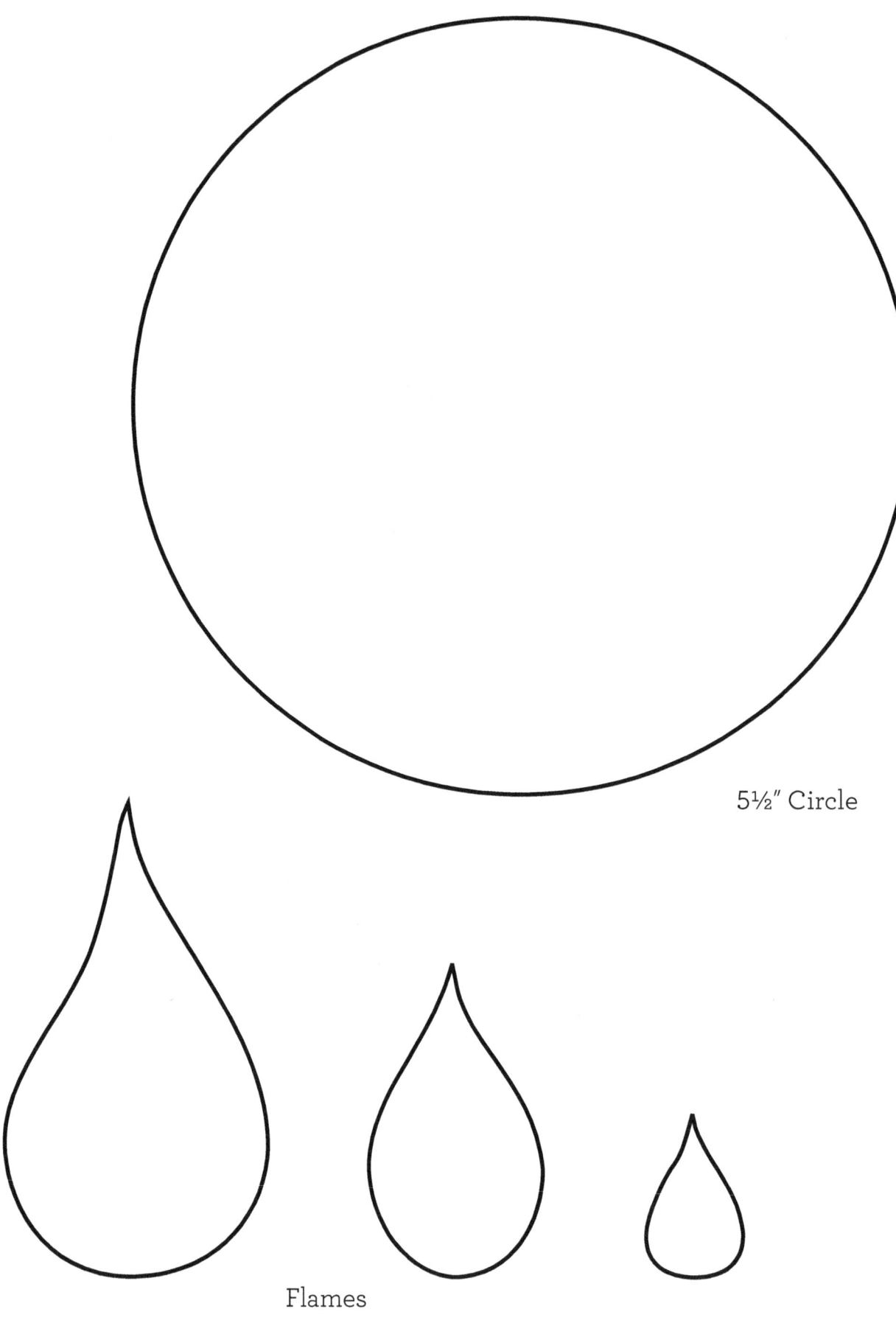

5½" Circle

Flames

16   Faith & Play™ | Images of God

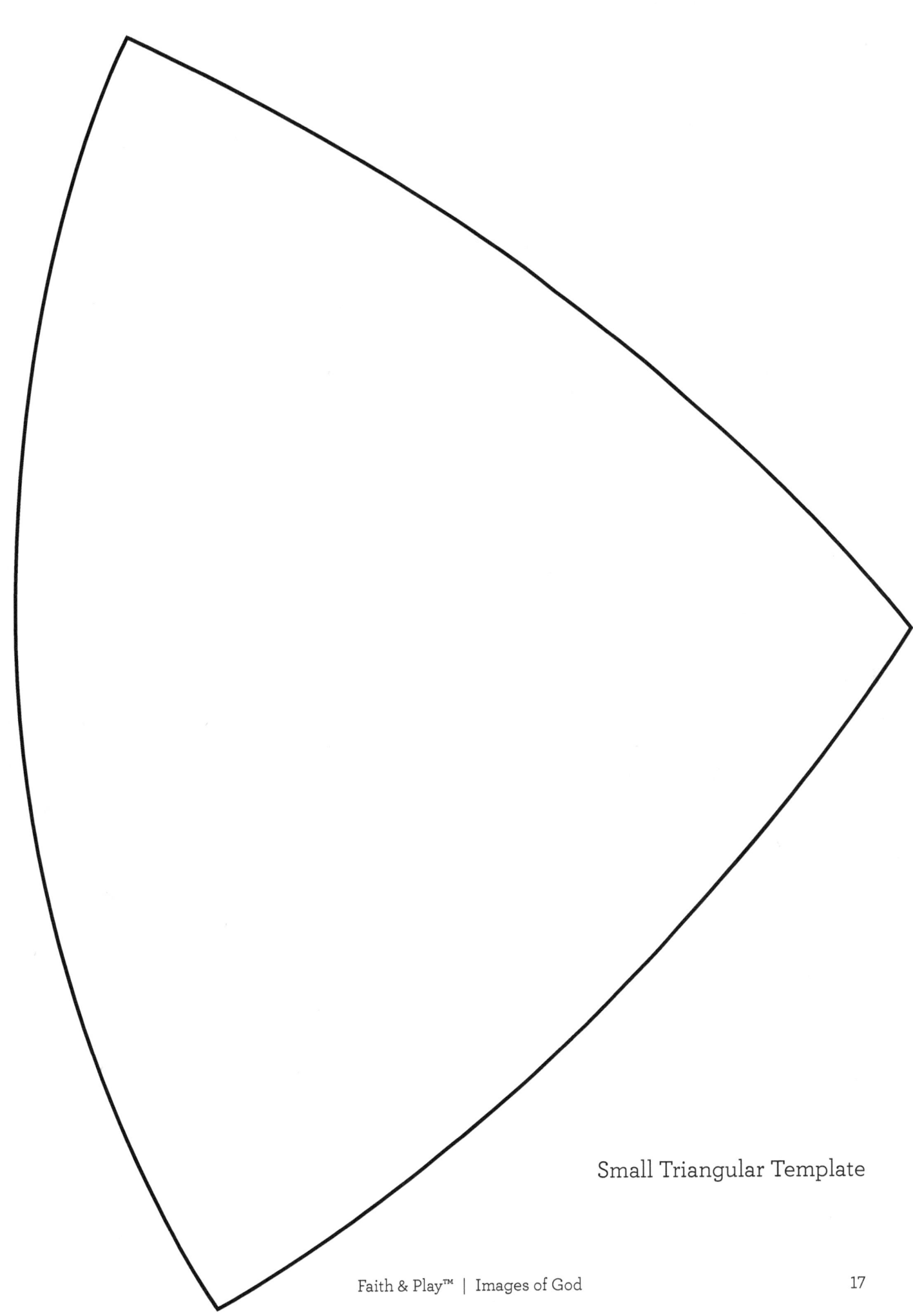

Small Triangular Template

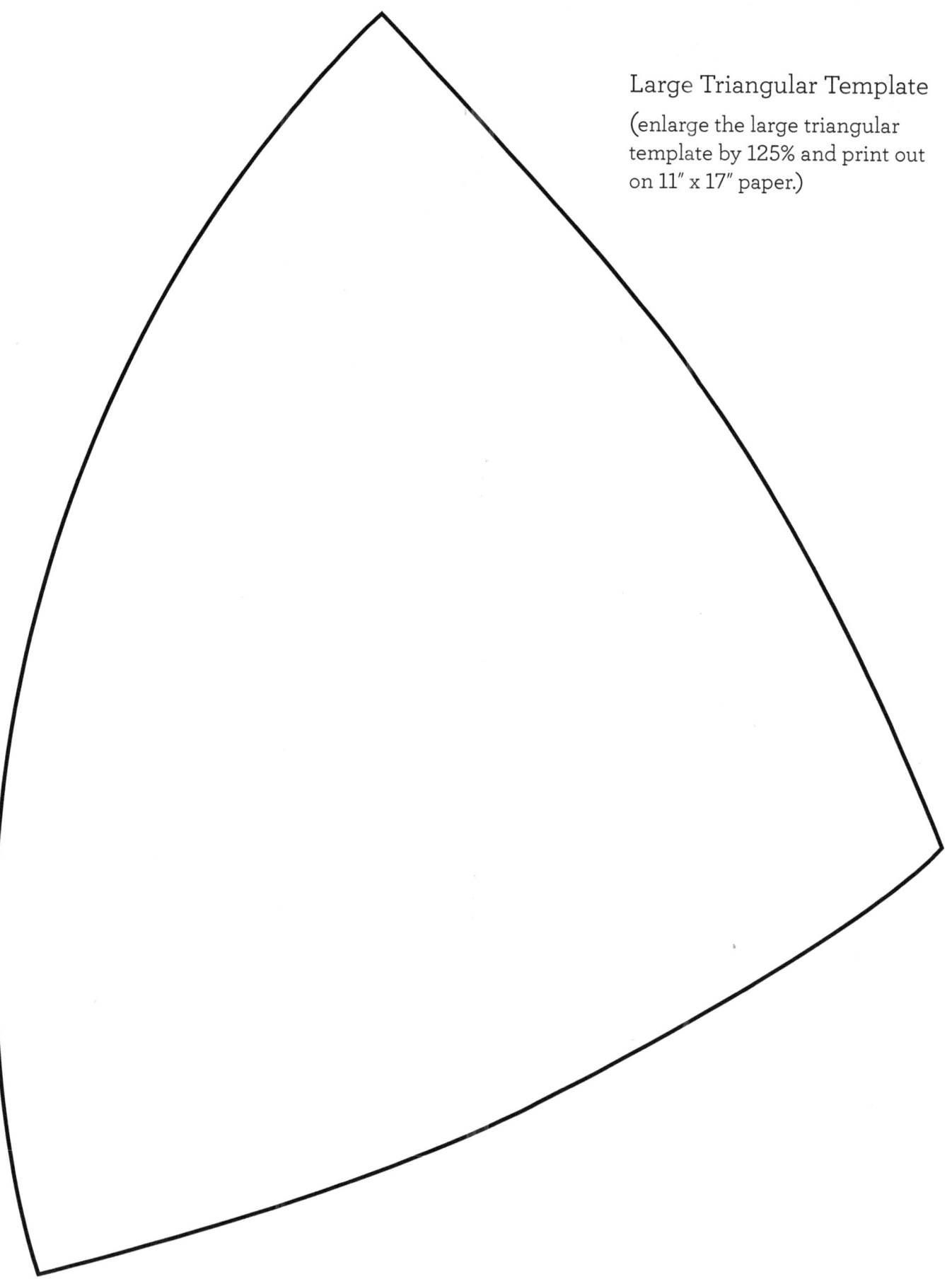

Large Triangular Template

(enlarge the large triangular template by 125% and print out on 11" x 17" paper.)

Breath Template

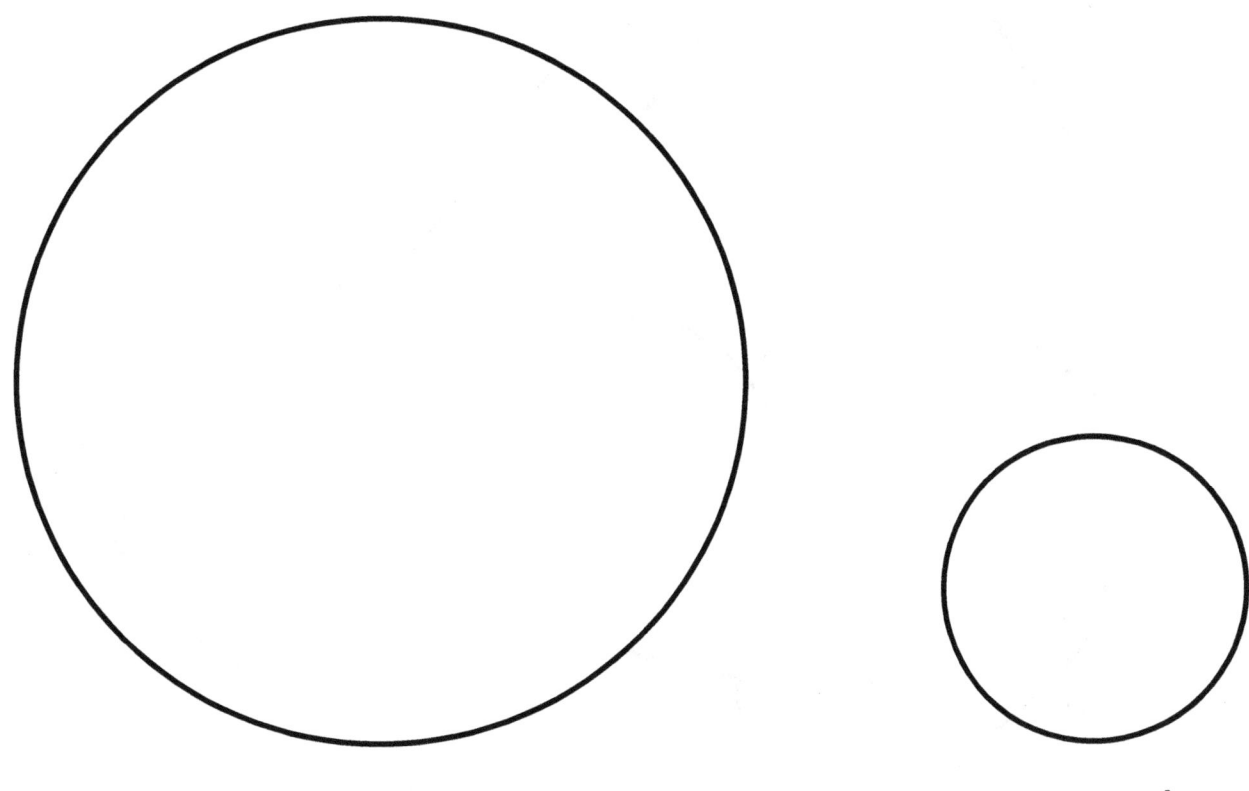

Compass Template

Inner Circle

Faith & Play™ | Images of God

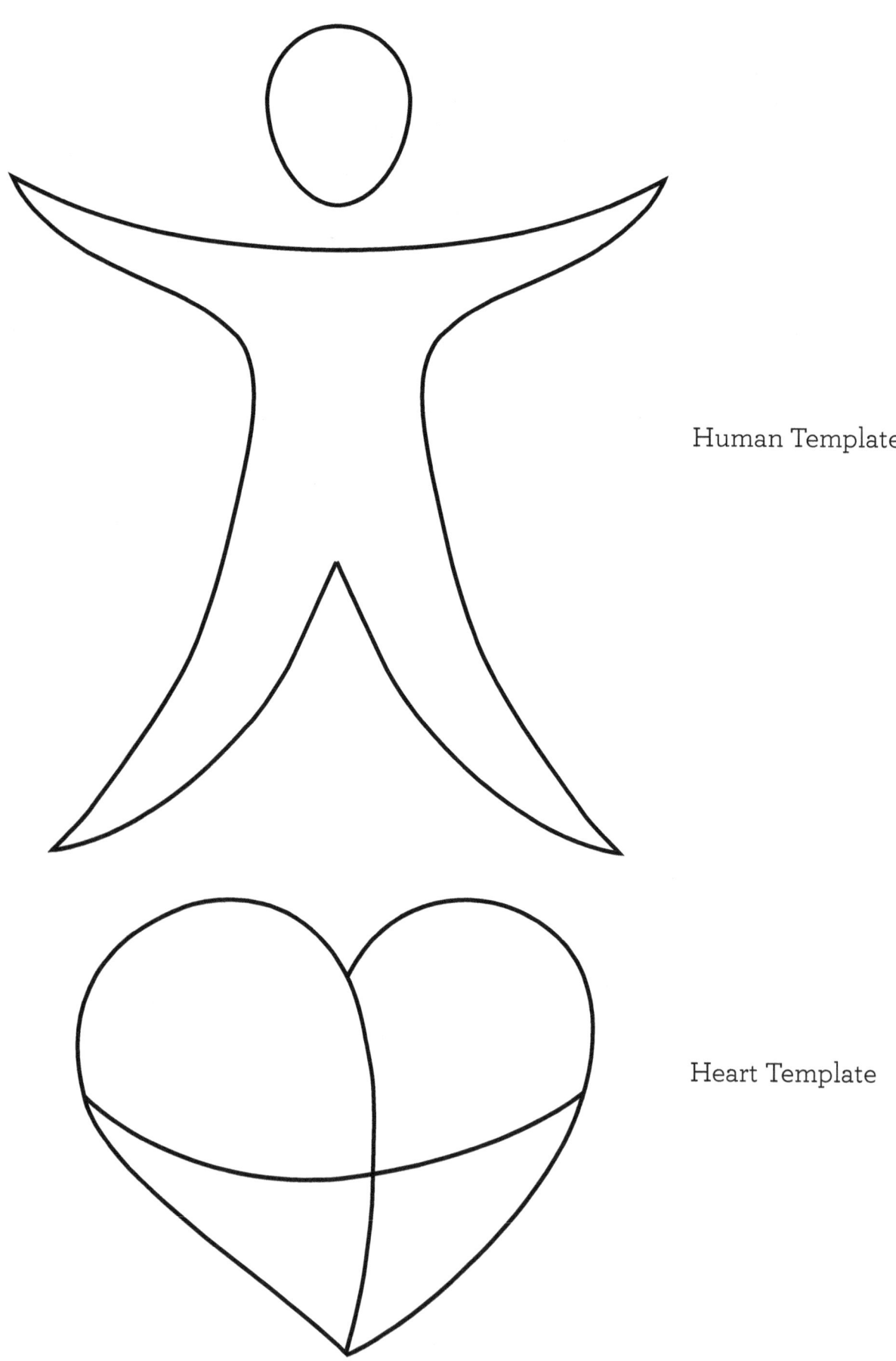

Human Template

Heart Template

Prayer and Friends Meeting for Worship

A story about Friends gathering as a community to listen for God

Photo taken from perspective of the listeners.

Materials

- A round red underlay, about 18" in diameter.
- A hard surface such as a shallow upside-down wooden box, a box lid, or a smooth piece of wood about 9" x 12".
- Six or more free-standing people figures with a red dot painted on each (on the chest).
- An archway or doorway large enough for the people figures to pass through one at a time. (This can be made of wood or clay.)
- A circle of red felt about 5" in diameter to be placed in the center of the meetinghouse.

The board or other smooth hard surface is the meetinghouse, and the arch is the door to the worship space. The red, suggesting fire, represents God's Spirit. The story materials may be kept in a basket, or, if the board will not fit in the story basket, you can simply put the basket on top of the board.

> NOTE: This story may be told as one lesson or as two. Lesson one focuses on the practice of individual prayer, and lesson two describes the experience of listening for God together in meeting for worship. If used as two lessons, stop the first time at the asterisk, then ask the wondering questions marked with asterisks.

WORDS

[*Optional*: Watch where I go to get this story so you will always know where to find it. It's not where the sacred stories are. It's not where the parables are.]

This is a Quaker story about prayer and Friends meeting for worship.

It is sometimes difficult to talk about God. We don't always know how to say what we feel and know inside. These are the best words I have at this time.

In each person — in you and in me — there is a deep, deep place. It is a special place where God is at home. It is also where we are at home with God.

Here is a deep, deep place. Here it is a tiny spot of color to remind us of a fire that always burns. Of course we can't really see it, but it is there.

The deep, deep place where God is at home in us and where we are at home in God.

Deep calls to deep. We hunger for God. God hungers for us. When we stop and listen, in prayer and in wonder, we know God is everywhere.

God is here.

MOVEMENTS

Get story materials from the Quaker story area and return to your place in the circle. Put story materials beside you.

Pause.

On the words "deep, deep place," put both hands, palms down, on the overlay.

Picking up a people figure, hold it lovingly, then gently indicate the red dot. Place the figure in front of you to the far left or right.

Pick up another figure, indicate the dot, then place it several inches from the first one. Silently point to the red dot on each remaining figure as you place them, one-by-one, in a semicircle with the open side toward you.

Place hands, palms down, on overlay on the words "deep calls to deep."

Indicate the red dot on each figure.

And God is here.	*Open your arms as if embracing the story space.*
God is everywhere and fills all. God never ends. There is always more.	*Spread arms out to your side.*
Even when we can't feel God, God is with us and in us and around us. God loves us. God helps us love. God is love.	
Sometimes we talk to God. We can tell God anything, and sometimes God talks to us. Most of all, though, we listen in the stillness. This is called prayer.	*Place a figure in one hand and gently cup the other hand a couple of inches above it.*
We can pray anywhere, at any time, and God always listens with love. We may say thank you or I love you. We may say I'm angry, God, or I'm afraid, or — help!	
Sometimes we spend time with God without using any words. This is prayer, too. There are many, many ways to pray. However we pray, deep calls to deep.*	*Lay the figure down on an open palm. Gently rock the figure in your outstretched hands like a cradle. Return figure to its place and lay hand on the underlay on "deep calls to deep."*

*If ending here, skip to the wondering questions.

Friends pray *together*, too. And when we come together to wait for God as a community, this is called meeting for worship. We wait in silence, in wonder and in love, in great expectation. We can do this in any place and at any time, but most often in a Friends meetinghouse.	
Here is a meetinghouse ... We prepare for worship throughout the week, then we come together. We are silent and still ... Deep calls to deep.	*Place hard surface and arch in front of you inside the semi-circle of figures. The arch should be centered near the edge of the board on the side closest to you. Slowly move each figure to the arch, pause, then move it through the arch until all of them are in a circle on the board. Make sure the red dots all face toward the center. Briefly wait in silence before proceeding. (Pausing at the door replicates our pausing before entering the Godly Play classroom. We enter when we are "ready.")*

Sometimes when Quakers worship together nothing special seems to happen. But God is still with us, loving us. We listen and pray.

Sometimes we sense God's presence in us and among us, and over us like a blanket of love that we all share as we worship. We call this a covered meeting.

God's presence. Hmm... Different worshippers may experience this in different ways.

This person feels it as a fire that never goes out, this one as an ocean of light.

This person feels God's presence as the water in a deep well, this one as the biggest hug that ever was, this one as wind.

This person has no words or images for the presence of God, but only a deep knowing.

This child has not yet learned how to speak. We do not know how he experiences God, but some day he may tell us.

This person is not sure she believes in God, but she knows that in meeting for worship something special happens that she cannot explain.

I do not know your experience of God's presence. Only you know that.

In worship we listen very carefully. Sometimes a person feels something happening inside that won't go away. That person listens very hard to answer questions inside:

"Is this from God or from somewhere else?

Is this for me only, or for the group?

If it is for everyone, do I share it now or later?"

Pause.

Place small red felt disk in center of the circle of figures. Place hands over the circle of figures, palms down, forming a "dome" of blessing over the meeting room.

Indicate each figure as you describe what each one experiences in worship.

Gently cup one or both hands over a figure.

Sometimes the person feels words inside that *are* from God, that *are* for everyone, and that *are* for now. Then the person shares the message in a clear voice so everyone can hear the message. The messenger uses as few words as possible and as many as needed, then stops and reenters the silence.	*Move the figure slightly forward, pause, then move it back on "reenters the silence."*
Deep calls to deep.	
Sometimes in worship God gathers us together. God comes so close to us,	*Lower both hands, palms down and cupped, in downward motion toward the people figures.*
and we come so close to God . . .	*Move hands, palms up, upward from the people figures.*
and we come so close to one another that we can see God in each other. We call this a gathered meeting.	*Make a holding, embracing gesture with both arms around the figures.*
After a while, the person caring for the meeting that day senses it is time to end meeting for worship. This person then shakes someone's hand. Everyone shakes hands. This is called rise of meeting.	*Move two figures together. Move each figure toward the nearest figure in pairs, then return them to their place in the circle.*
Then it is time for announcements, the time to share what is happening in the meeting community.	
After saying good-bye we go out of the meetinghouse and take our love into the world. We continue to listen and pray.	*Pass the figures through the arch and place them on the floor in a semi-circle as before.*
And even when we are far apart we are never alone. For God is always with us and we are always part of God's family.	
	Pause. When you begin the wondering, look up at participants to indicate you welcome their responses.
I wonder what part of this story you like best.*	[*It is not appropriate to use all of these wondering questions each time, but as participants begin to respond you can get a sense of what wonderings are the right ones for the group at this time. An appropriate wondering might arise that is not listed here.]*
I wonder what part of this story is most important to you right now.*	
I wonder where and when you have prayed.*	

I wonder what kinds of places we can pray or worship.

I wonder what you do in meeting for worship.

I wonder what image you might use to describe your experience of God's presence.

I wonder what image you might use to describe your experience of meeting for worship.

I wonder when you have seen God in someone else.

I wonder if you have ever had the experience of a gathered or covered meeting.

Have you heard or shared a message in meeting? I wonder what that was like for you.

I wonder what you could do to prepare for meeting for worship.

I wonder what part of this story we can leave out, and still have all the story we need.

I wonder what you wonder about this story.*

Note to storytellers:

The phrase "Deep calls to deep" is from Psalm 42:7 New International Version (NIV): Deep calls to deep in the roar of your waterfalls; all your waves and breakers have swept over me.

The threshold suggested in the materials, and shown in the picture here, may not represent the entrance/threshold in all the places where we gather for worship. You are invited to adapt the "threshold" to reflect your worship space and how it is entered by the community; try to keep these materials simple, and the focus on crossing into holy space.

Friends whose worship is semi-programmed or programmed will need to make adaptations to reflect the practices in your worship.

You could conclude the story by distributing small red felt disks saying something like, "May this remind you of that deep, deep place where God is at home in you and where you are at home in God." These disks may be kept in a small, attractive cardboard or wooden box with the story materials.

Additional Resources for Exploring Waiting Worship with Children:

Quaker Meeting and Me: a guide for children attending worship at Quaker meetings and churches, Quaker Religious Education Collaborative, illustrations by Rebecca Price, 2017. (QMandM@quakers4re.org)

We're Going to Meeting for Worship, Abby A. Hadley, Friends General Conference, 2006. (www.quakerbooks.org)

First Day Stories, Katherine K. Newman, 2017. (www.quakerbooks.org)

Friends Meeting for Business

A story about meeting for worship with attention to business

Materials

The materials for the Faith & Play story *Prayer and Friends Meeting for Worship* are used for this story. Make sure you have at least six adult figures for this story.

WORDS	MOVEMENTS
[*Optional*: Watch where I go to get this story so you will always know where to find it. It's not where the sacred stories are. It's not where the parables are.]	*Get story materials from the Quaker story area and return to your place in the circle.*
This is a Quaker story about when Friends gather to have a meeting for business.	
	Put story materials beside you. Get out the red underlay and smooth it out. Set up the meetinghouse and place people figures outside it in a semi-circle on the red underlay.
Each week, Friends gather as a community for meeting for worship. Once a month, we also meet together to take care of the business of the meeting community.	*Move the figures into the meetinghouse space and into a circle as in Prayer and Friends Meeting for Worship.*
Just as Friends gather in this space to listen for God in worship, we gather here to listen for God in meeting for worship with attention to business.	
Two Friends have a special care for this meeting. This Friend is the clerk of the meeting. Her job is to listen for how the Spirit is working in the meeting community. The clerk is listening to Friends all week long, all month long, between these meetings. She helps the meeting community know what business they need to work on each month.	*Pick up the clerk figure. Cradle the figure in your hand, and speak about him/her lovingly.*
	Place figure back in the circle.

Another job Friends share is serving as the recording clerk for the meeting. This person listens and writes down how the Spirit is working in the meeting, and records what decisions are made. We call these notes minutes, and they are like the history of our meeting community.

Pick up the recording clerk figure. Cradle the figure in your hand, and speak about him/her lovingly.

Place figure back in the circle.

When Friends take care of our meeting's business, we are holding the whole meeting in the Light. We enter into worship and we listen. We listen for God, we listen in our own hearts, and we listen to one another to know what to do.

Hold your hands around the circle of Friends.

Sometimes Friends make decisions about taking care of the meetinghouse or someone in our community. Sometimes we are deciding how to work for peace, or who will get ready for a meeting supper [potluck, event]. There are so many jobs to do and decisions to make.

Today, in this meeting for business, Friends have a concern about their meetinghouse property. Outside the meetinghouse is a very old tree. The tree's roots are sick and the tree is no longer living and growing. The meeting must decide what to do about the tree.

The clerk asks the Friends who serve on the Property Committee what they recommend. This group of Friends helps to care for the meetinghouse and its land. They asked a tree doctor what to do.

A Friend from the Property Committee stands, and speaks clearly. He uses as few words as possible yet as many as are needed. The committee recommends that the tree be cut down. It might fall and hurt someone or damage the meetinghouse if they don't cut it down.

Pick up a new figure, and hold in your hand with care.

Place figure back in the circle.

Faith & Play™ | Friends Meeting for Business

The clerk thanks the Property Committee for their work and their recommendation. Now there is time for Friends to share how the Spirit is leading them in this decision.

Another Friend speaks. He remembers climbing this tree when he was a boy, and he will be sad to see it cut down. It feels like losing a member of the meeting community.   *Indicate a Friend in the circle.*

This Friend feels strongly that the tree needs to be removed. What if it fell on a car, or damaged the building?   *Indicate a Friend in the circle.*

The clerk asks Friends if they might settle into worship to listen inwardly for way to open. They need to find unity, the feeling that the meeting has been led by Spirit to a decision together.

Out of the silence, this Friend shares an idea: perhaps, if the tree is cut down, the wood might be given to a family in need of firewood for the winter.   *Indicate a Friend in the circle.*

Out of worship, this Friend shares that perhaps, in the spring, the First Day School class could plant a new tree in the place of the tree they need to cut down.   *Indicate a Friend in the circle.*

Out of the stillness, this Friend stands and suggests that the meeting gather under the tree before worship next week, to share their memories and perhaps a song.   *Indicate a Friend in the circle.*

A sense of peace begins to settle into the meetinghouse.

The clerk, whose job it is to listen for how the Spirit is working, speaks out of the silence: the sense of the meeting is that it is the right decision to cut down the tree. The clerk affirms that Friends will also find ways to celebrate the tree's life. Meeting members are silent, but Friends smile or nod their heads in agreement.   *Gently indicate the clerk figure.*

Friends have reached unity on this concern.

Place the smaller red circle used in Prayer and Friends Meeting for Worship in the center of the circle of Friends.

The recording clerk minutes all of this.

Gently indicate the recording clerk figure.

After any other old or new business the meeting needs to attend to, Friends continue with a period of worship, and end with handshakes. They have listened for God. They have taken care of their meeting's business together. Spirit led the way.

Friends go out into the world to continue God's work. They take with them hearts that know love, peace, and unity.

Pass the figures back through the arch and place them on the floor in a semi-circle as they were at the start of the story.

Pause. When you begin the wondering, look up at participants to indicate you welcome their responses.

I wonder what part of the story you like best.

I wonder what part of the story is most important for you today.

I wonder where you are in the story, or what part is about you.

I wonder what part of the story we could leave out, and still have all the story we need.

I wonder when you have ever listened in your heart for what to do.

I wonder when you have ever made a decision with your family or friends, and felt a sense of unity.

Note to storytellers:

If the tree scenario is not appropriate to your meeting's situation or property, Friends are invited to consider another "item of business" when they share this story. If you decide to focus the story on an alternative item of business, remember to keep the focus on discernment and making room for Spirit and silence in that process. Model different points of view being heard (as in the published story about a property decision), but do not feel you need to fill the story with words to describe the experience.

Other options suggested by storytellers in our community:
- How to involve the children more in the life of the meeting? How many all-ages meetings for worship will we have this year? How can we make our meeting house and gardens a more interesting place for the children of the meeting?
- Approving a service project or community event hosted by the meeting.
- Nominating Committee business: everyone's gifts are needed in the meeting community.

Alternate Work with the Children:

In the work time after the story, one option is to have a meeting for business with the children. Provide a clear, but open-ended query or decision for them, and ask two children to take on the roles of clerk (calling on other children to speak) and recording clerk. Provide the recording clerk with paper, pencil, and a hard writing surface like a clipboard.

Children can think about a question or decision, like: "The adults working with First Day School are working on how to get ready for Christmas. What suggestions do you have for Christmas in our meeting this year?"

When children begin their meeting for business, give each of them one or two pieces of a large, red circle you have cut out of felt or paper ahead of time. When they are called on by the clerk to share, they place a piece of the "pie" in the center of the circle they are sitting in. When all ideas are shared, ask the recorder to read them back from the "minutes." Help the clerk to ask if there is unity about their ideas and what they have decided. If there is unity, add any remaining pieces to complete the red circle in the center of the children.

End with a period of silent worship.

Thank the children for their participation. Be sure to follow through with any decisions or suggestions that need to be shared with adults in the meeting community!

Gifts

A story about the gifts God gives each of us

Photo taken from perspective of the listeners.

Materials

- A dark blue, deep purple or black underlay, about 24″ square.
- Eight felt pieces in eight different colors that, when put together like a puzzle, create a large square or frame with an open circle in the center. (See patterns at end of this story.)
- Five wedge-shaped cutouts in medium blue felt, each with a cutout or painting of a human figure with outstretched arms. Each figure should be a different color to suggest

Faith & Play™ | Gifts 33

the diversity of our communities and the variety of gifts. These five pieces fit into the circle in the puzzle square in such a way that they reach towards each other with feet toward the center of the circle. The completed layout will look like a mosaic, quilt, or stained glass window. (See patterns at end of this story.)

SPECIAL NOTE: The optional text in brackets expands the story for use with older children or in some multigenerational settings.

WORDS

[*Optional*: Watch where I go to get this story so you will always know where to find it. It is not where the sacred stories are. It is not where the parables are.]

This is a Quaker story about gifts.

Gifts are very special things. Gifts can come wrapped in a colorful package with a bow. Birthday gifts. Christmas gifts. Gifts that say, "thank you." Gifts that say, "I love you." Gifts for no particular reason.

There are many other kinds of gifts. They are all around us. It can be something someone does for another person, like washing the dishes, or giving someone a hug. It can be something we don't even see, like the air we breathe.

Then there are the gifts that God gives to each one of us. Our gifts are special parts of who we are. These gifts help us live a whole life, make a whole family, or be a whole meeting community.

People young and old bring their gifts to our meeting community. If we pay attention and care for one another, we can discover them. We can help each other understand how to use those gifts wisely.

This person always makes people feel at home in the meeting. She greets everyone with a warm smile and sometimes a hug. She has a gift of welcome.

MOVEMENTS

Get story materials from the Quaker story area and return to your place in the circle. Put materials beside you.

Get out the underlay and smooth it out. Begin laying out the eight outer puzzle pieces, slowly and one at a time, as you speak.

Continue laying out puzzle pieces until the outer frame is completed.

Place one "pie slice" in the circle within the square. Gently indicate the human figure.

This gift is not for her alone. God gave it to her for the whole meeting community. Perhaps you know someone like her.

This one is always doing something for others. He sends birthday and get well cards to people. He bakes cookies for service projects. He helps to take care of the meetinghouse. He has a gift of service.

Place a second "pie slice" in the circle within the square. Gently indicate the human figure.

This gift is not for him alone. God gave it to him for the whole meeting community. Perhaps you know someone like him.

This one always has a good question. People find that her questions are often their questions, too. She helps everyone think about the things that really matter. She has a gift of questions.

Place a third "pie slice" in the circle within the square. Gently indicate the human figure.

This gift is not for her alone. God gave it to her for the whole meeting community. Perhaps you know someone like her.

This one loves music. His songs can turn frowns into smiles and make people happy. Sometimes his songs are so beautiful everyone is quiet and still. He has a gift of song.

Place a fourth "pie slice" in the circle within the square. Gently indicate the human figure.

This gift is not for him alone. God gave it to him for the whole meeting community. Perhaps you know someone like him.

This one isn't sure what her gifts are. Sometimes it takes a long time to understand our gifts. She will listen in her heart; she will listen for God. Her meeting community will help her discover and use her gifts. Perhaps you know someone like her.

Place the last "pie slice" in the circle within the square. Gently indicate the human figure.

In our meeting community God gives us all the gifts we need.

Make a circular motion with your hand moving from figure to figure.

[*Optional*: One day the meeting decided to invite people of different religions, or faiths, to the meetinghouse. They hoped to get Jews, Muslims and Christians together to have fun and work for peace. The meeting members put their gifts together.

Faith & Play™ | Gifts

This person said, "I'll help set up the tables and chairs."	*Indicate the second "pie slice" figure by touching, tilting upward, or gently lifting.*
This one said, "I'll greet everyone when they arrive."	*Similarly indicate the first "pie slice" figure,*
This one said, "I know a song about peace I can sing. Then we can all sing it together."	*then the fourth "pie slice" figure,*
This one said, "I will find some good queries and discussion questions to help us get to know one another."	*then the third "pie slice" figure.*

Another person offered to print the invitation letters. Someone offered to send them out. Someone else offered to make snacks. Everyone worked together. But one person was silent. What gift would she bring?

The next week, this person said, "I know a fun game I can teach everyone. It is a game where nobody loses. It's a fun peace game."	*Indicate the fifth "pie slice" figure.*
In time, the meeting community learned that this one has a gift of joy and laughter. Everyone helped her to see this gift. And she learned that the gift is not for her alone, but for the whole meeting community.]	*Pick up the fifth figure and lovingly hold it towards the listeners.* *Place the figure back in the circle.*
God gives gifts to each one of us. Our gifts are parts of who we are. God works in our hearts and through our gifts. Our meeting community (or family) has all the gifts we need. Thank you, God.	*Indicate each figure briefly, palm down, as in blessing. Then make circular motion with hands, palms up, encompassing all of the figures.* *Pause. When you begin the wondering, look up at participants to indicate you welcome their responses.*

I wonder what part of this story you like best.

I wonder what part is most important for you today.

I wonder what gifts you have discovered in our meeting [or in our group].

I wonder where you are in the story.

I wonder what gifts God has given you for the community.

I wonder how we might show our thanks for the gifts God has given our meeting [or our group].

> ALTERNATE GIFT TEXT: The script as written will likely be adequate for many settings, but two alternative gift descriptions are offered for your use, should one or both of them be more fitting to your setting. You may customize the story to your environment, if you like, by creating one or two new gift descriptions of your own to replace the same number in the story.

This one is always doing something around the meetinghouse. He (or she) makes shelves for the classroom. He cuts the grass. He fixes the meetinghouse door when it is broken. He has a gift of practical service.

This gift is not for him alone. God gave it to him for the whole meeting community. Perhaps you know someone like him. [In the earlier bracketed portion of the story, this character can set up chairs or tables, make sure the grass is cut and the shrubbery trimmed, or do anything else that could be considered "practical service."]

This one loves children. Her (or his) heart smiles whenever she sees young people in the meeting. She understands children, and loves to exchange stories with them. Children feel at home with her. Her gift is a natural ease with children.

This gift is not for her alone. God gave it to her for the whole meeting community. Perhaps you know someone like her. [In the earlier bracketed portion of the story, this character might say, "I will play with the children."]

Note to storytellers:

This story is grounded in Paul's First Letter to the Corinthians, Chapter 12:4-11 New International Version (NIV):

4 There are different kinds of gifts, but the same Spirit distributes them. 5 There are different kinds of service, but the same Lord. 6 There are different kinds of working, but in all of them and in everyone it is the same God at work. 7 Now to each one the manifestation of the Spirit is given for the common good. 8 To one there is given through the Spirit a message of wisdom, to another a message of knowledge by means of the same Spirit, 9 to another faith by the same Spirit, to another gifts of healing by that one Spirit, 10 to another miraculous powers, to another prophecy, to another distinguishing between spirits, to another speaking in different kinds of tongues,[a] and to still another the interpretation of tongues. 11 All these are the work of one and the same Spirit, and he distributes them to each one, just as he determines.

We also offer this quotation from American theologian James Fowler (1940-2015):

"We become true individuals only in community, in relation to God and neighbor. In community we discover our gifts and our call."

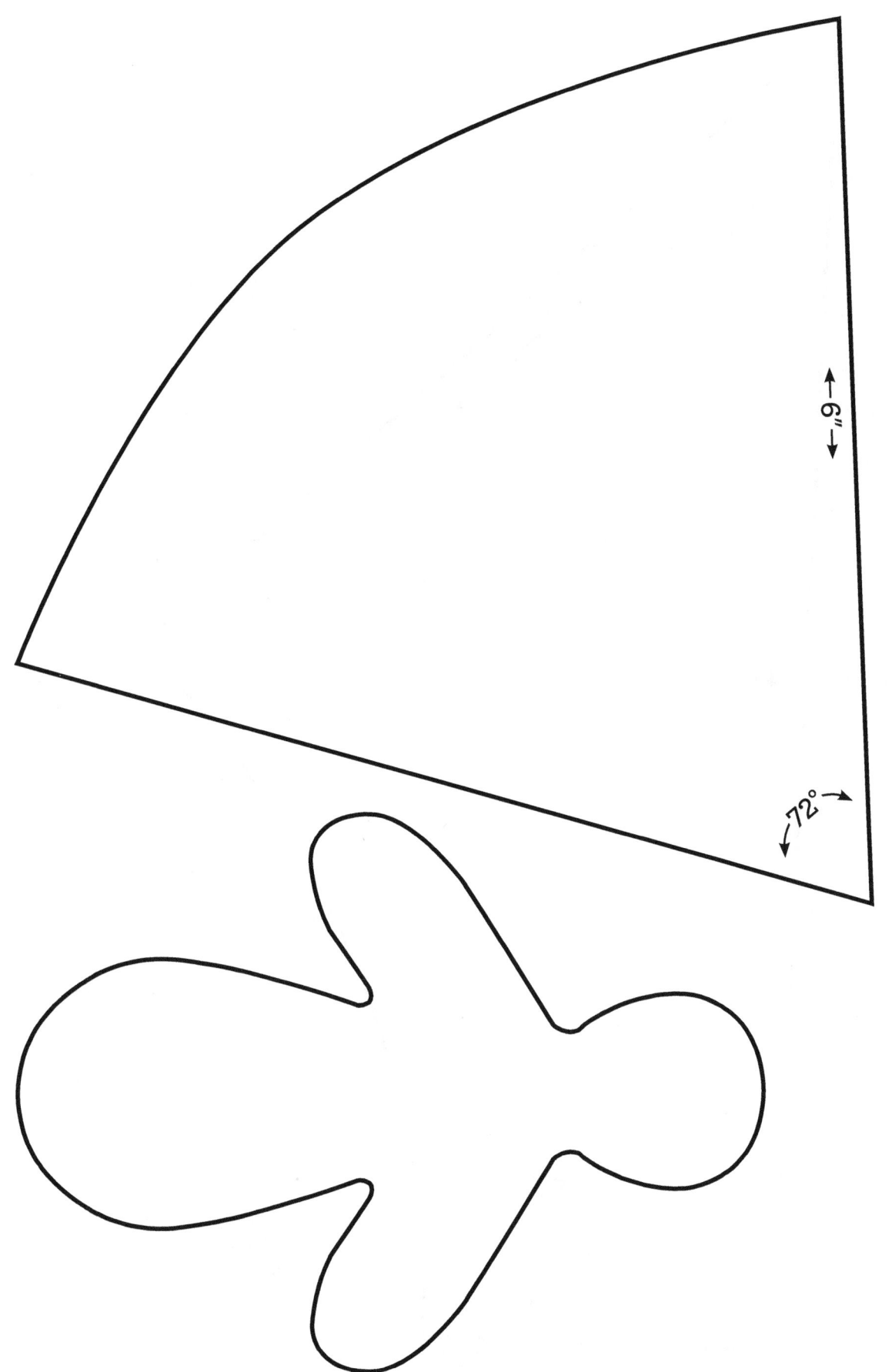

Faith & Play™ | Gifts

39

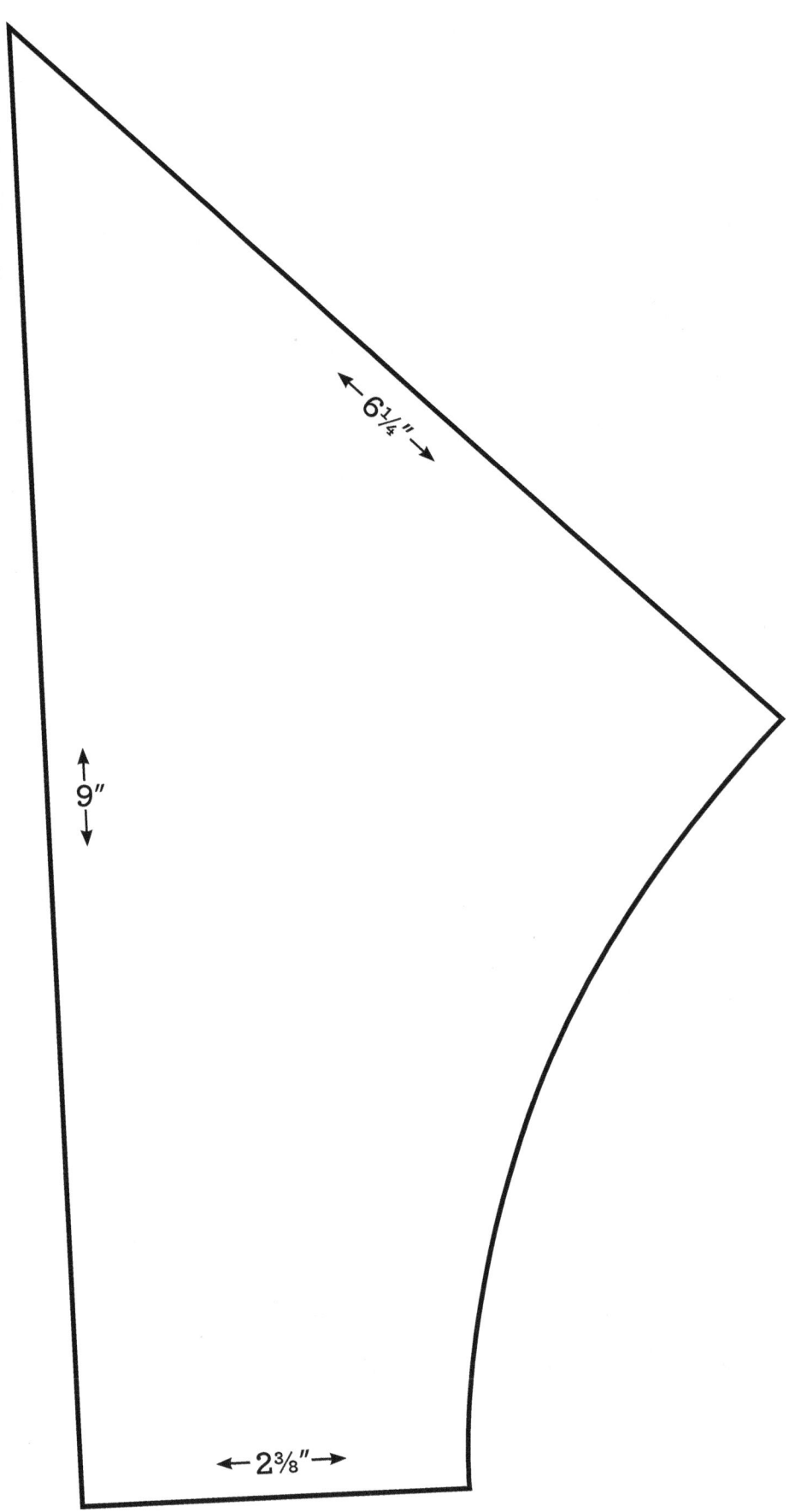

Queries

A story about the role of queries for early and present-day Quakers

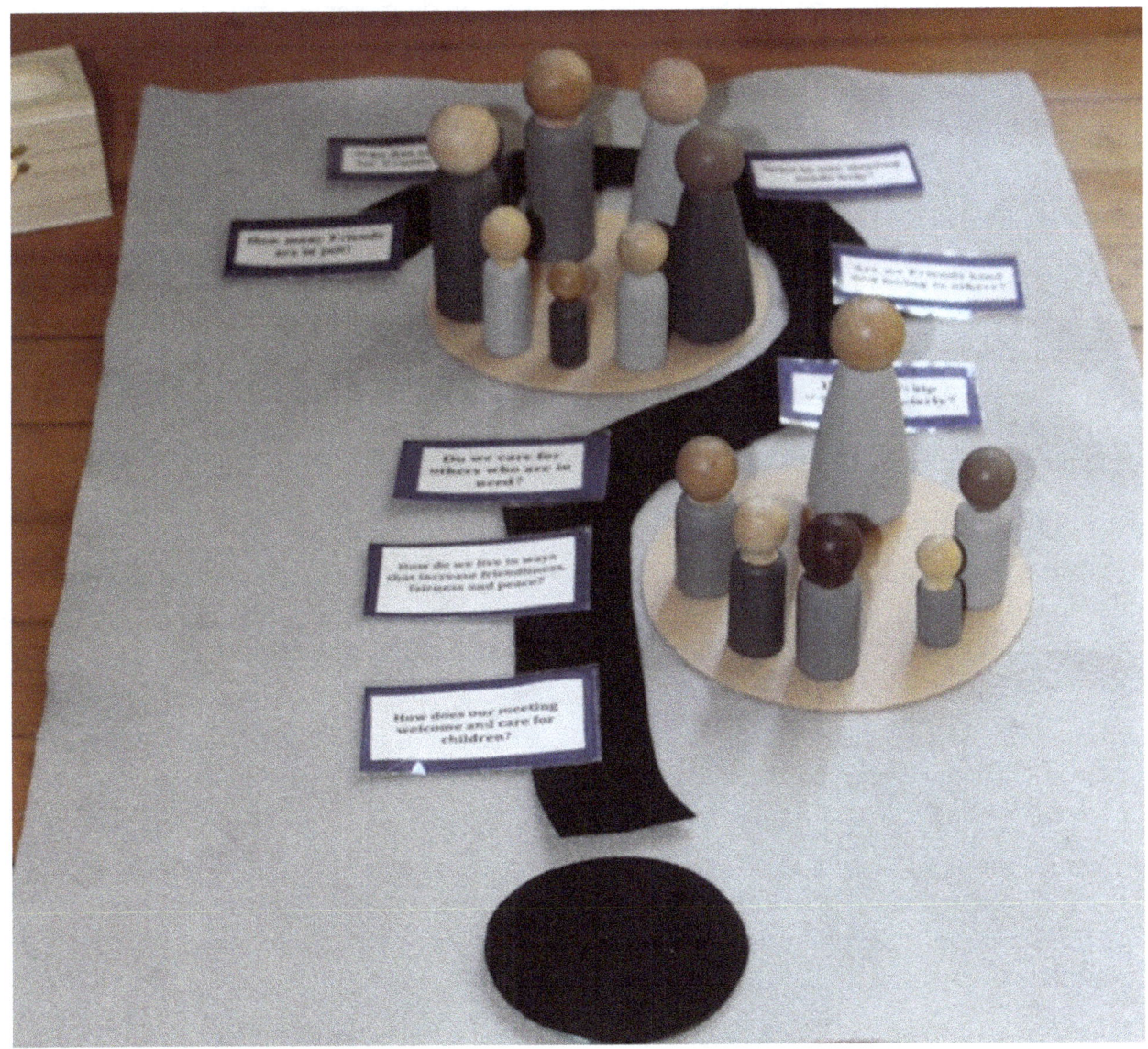

Photo taken from perspective of the listeners.

Materials

- A light blue or grey felt underlay, approximately 18" x 24".
- Two tan felt circles about 5½" in diameter (one representing a contemporary First Day program for children, and the other, a circle of early Friends).
- Six or more freestanding people figures representing the contemporary children and adult.

Faith & Play™ | Queries

41

- Six or more additional people figures representing historic Friends.
- A dark blue or black felt question mark that fits on the underlay, and is large enough to encircle the historic Friends at its top. The question mark, minus the dot, is 18" from top edge to bottom edge. It can either be a single piece that is unrolled during the story (as noted in the movements) or be constructed in three sections which are laid down sequentially as story is told.
- The dot at the end of the question mark is about 3" in diameter. A small, circular mirror is adhered to one side.
- Eight queries (see templates). These query cards are cut out and may be laminated and/or mounted on card stock. See story for order of query cards along question mark.

OPTIONAL: To make a jail, use felt, stiff felt, or craft foam, and cut out a barred window.

WORDS	MOVEMENTS
[*Optional*: Watch where I go to get this story so you will always know where to find it. It is not where the sacred stories are. It is not where the parables are.]	*Get story materials from the Quaker story area and return to your place in the circle. Put story materials beside you.*
This is a Quaker story about queries.	
Questions are important. We ask and answer questions every day. Here is a child. Everywhere that she goes people ask her questions.	*Remove underlay from basket, smoothing it out with care. Take one child figure from the basket, and place on the surface.*
At home, her parents ask her questions such as these: "Did you sleep well? Could you help me with this? "Why did you do that?"	*Look at figure, directing the questions to it.*
At school, the child's teacher asks questions, as well. "Have you finished your project? Did you do your best work? Will you please help us clean up?"	*Move figure to slightly different position on underlay to represent being at school.*
Questions are important. On Sundays, the child goes to Friends Meeting with her family. Before beginning the story, the First Day School teachers ask a question, "Are you ready?" and after the story," I wonder what your work will be today?"	*Place one tan circle on underlay to lower left of storyteller. Place Anna figure on the circle, then add the other child figures with it in a semi-circle, facing the circle of children in your class. Hold teacher figure(s) up in your hand, then place them in the circle facing you.*

Now, there is a curious and wonderful thing about questions. The same question can have different answers for different people. It is true that there are some questions that have only one right answer. Questions such as, "What is one plus one?"

Hold up index finger of each hand to indicate "one plus one."

But some of the best questions in the world do not have one right answer. And the answer that is right for you or me might change over time.

Something else about questions—there are different ways of answering them. Often questions are answered with words, but sometimes with actions, pictures, or dreams.

This child draws a picture to answer a question. This child answers with a daydream. This child answers with words, this child, by working with clay.

Gently touch different child figures as you talk about the different ways of answering.

Sometimes, there are questions that we just can't answer. Maybe we're not ready yet, but we keep listening. There are so many places where we ask and answer questions.

Questions were important to the first Friends, or Quakers.

Place second tan circle to the upper right from storyteller's perspective. Place six people figures (adults and children) representing early Friends in a circle on the tan felt.

Friends believed that God could be found in the heart of every person. Every person. So the Friends would not carry weapons, or fight in wars, or show special treatment to people with riches or titles.

Because of these beliefs and actions, early Friends were sometimes put in jail and treated badly.

Move two figures out of circle to storyteller's right. If used, lean cut-out of jail in front of the two figures. The storyteller can also use their hand in front of the figures to denote jail bars.

Now, it was because of this, and in order to help one another, that early Friends began to ask themselves particular questions, which they called inquiries or queries. The first queries were questions such as these:

"How many Friends are in jail?"
"Who has suffered for Truth's sake?"
"Who in our meeting needs help?"

Take rolled-up felt question mark, place on your right next to the circle of early Friends and unroll part way until question mark is most of the way around the tan circle. Alternately, place first of three question mark sections around circle of early Friends. (See photo. The question mark will eventually encircle the early Friends, and then partly encircle the children and teacher figures.) Hold up each query card as you speak it, and then place each along the top portion of the question mark.

These first queries were the sort of questions that could be answered with names and numbers. After answering them, the people of the meeting could go out and give help. These queries were important to Friends. Answering them was a way of helping one another.

Return jailed Friends to circle, and jail, if used, to story tray.

The queries that Friends asked themselves changed over time, but answering them was still a way of helping one another. Friends began to ask themselves queries about how well they were living out their belief that God is in the heart of every person, queries such as these:

Unroll question mark until it completely encircles early Friends figures. Alternately, place second section of question mark on underlay.

Are we Friends kind and loving to others?
Do we worship together regularly?
Do we care for others who are in need?

Place each query card on question mark as you speak it.

At first, Friends thought there was only one right answer to particular queries. If your answer were not the right one, then you might have to leave your meeting. At the time, Friends thought this was the right way.

Touch a figure in Friends circle whose answer is not "right." Move this figure out of the circle, to storyteller's right on underlay.

Over time, the right way for Friends changed. Queries came to be the kind of questions where different people may have different answers, even if there is one answer that is considered to be the best.

Return figure to Friends circle.

For hundreds of years, Friends have kept on asking themselves queries about how well they are living out their faith.

Continue to unroll question mark slowly, until it is complete. Alternately, place third piece on underlay to complete the question mark.

Some queries are for each of us to ask ourselves—queries such as:

Hold up the dot with the mirror side toward the listeners and then place at bottom of question mark with the mirror side up before sharing queries.

"Do you live in a way that increases friendliness, fairness and peace?"

Place each query on the question mark as you speak it.

Other queries are for the Meeting community to work on together, queries such as: "Does your meeting welcome and care for children?"

Friends here at _____ (*name your meeting*) ask ourselves queries to this very day. To answer them, we listen in our hearts, we listen for God, we listen to one another.

Place hands on your heart. Then stretch out your arms with your hands cupped, palms up; then put cupped hands around story figures.

Pause. When you begin the wondering, look up at participants to indicate you welcome their responses.

I wonder what part of this story you like best.

I wonder what part is most important for you right now.

I wonder if there is any part we could leave out and still have all the story we need.

I wonder where you are in this story, or what part of the story is about you.

I wonder if you've ever had a question or a query that you just couldn't answer.

I wonder how you try to find answers to your questions.

I wonder what it feels like to work on a query together.

I wonder what questions are important to you.

You might pick up the mirror and hold out toward listeners as you ask this wondering question.

Optional query response for older children during work time:

What is most important to you in your life right now?

Draw or write your answer in private, and we will put it in this envelope. I will give you your answer at the end of the year. (Note: The teacher may choose to offer wood and clay, as well, as ways of responding to this query. In this case, you will want to put the answers in a box, rather than an envelope.)

How many
Friends are in jail?

Who has suffered
for Truth's sake?

Who in our meeting
needs help?

Are we Friends kind
and loving to others?

Do we worship
together regularly?

Do we care for others
who are in need?

How do we live in ways that increase
friendliness, fairness and peace?

How does our meeting welcome
and care for children?

*Slight variation on last query
for Friends school setting:*

How does our school welcome
and include everyone?

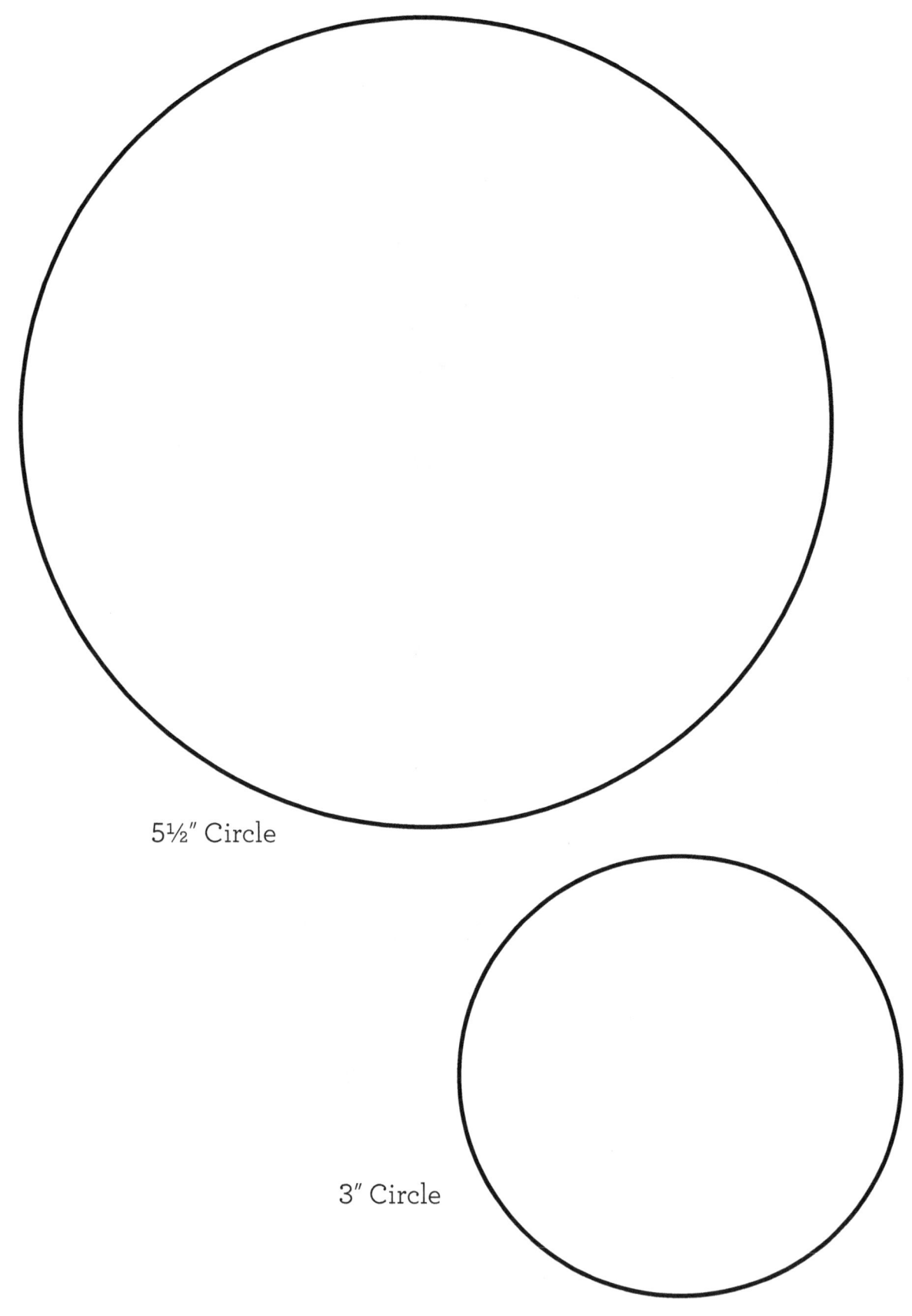

5½" Circle

3" Circle

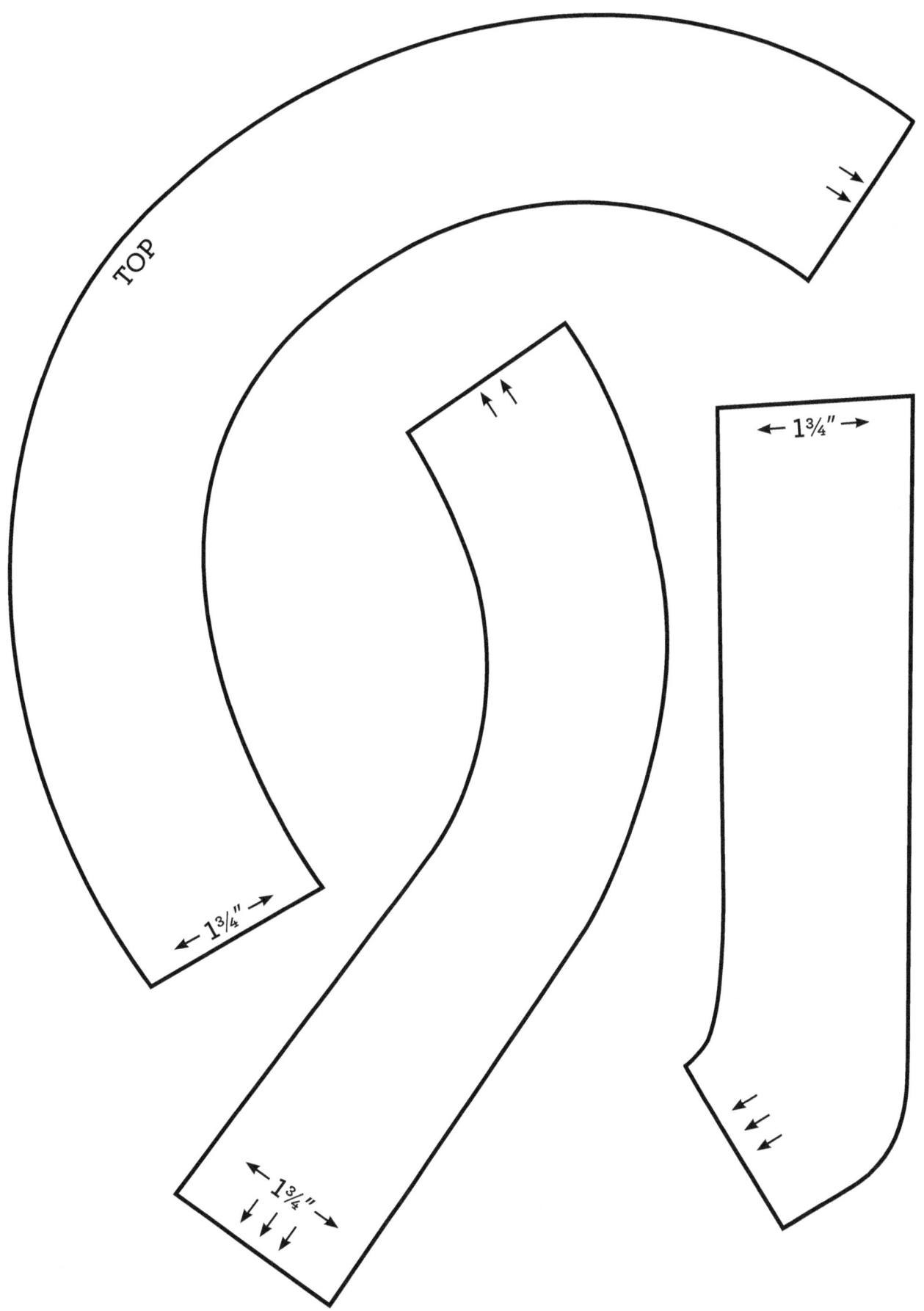

Faith & Play™ | Queries

Stories about the Testimonies

Love's Way

A story about testimonies for younger children

Photo taken from perspective of the listeners.

Materials

- a circle of medium blue felt about 24" in diameter (the underlay)
- a single flame graphic about 3½–4" high made of successive layers of orange, yellow and red felt, with each of the three layers smaller than the previous one
- a red felt disk about 5½" in diameter (the flame is placed on top of the disk) (See templates for flame and circle in Appendices.)
- six wooden hearts about 5" wide
- wooden graphics to glue onto each of the hearts to represent testimonies of simplicity, integrity, peace, equality, community, and stewardship. Here are suggested graphics: a

Faith & Play™ | Love's Way

small heart (integrity), a person figure with arms extended and holding a small gold heart (simplicity), a dove cutout (peace), two people cutouts in different colors placed side by side (equality), three to five flat people figures also in different colors and arranged in a circle (community), and a small earth (stewardship).

- six similarly sized 3-dimensional wooden or clay people figures in three or four different shades (or colors) and shapes, each with a red dot or oval painted on each chest

WORDS	MOVEMENTS
[*Optional*: Watch where I go to get this story so you will always know where to find it. It's not where the sacred stories are. It's not where the parables are.]	*Go to story materials and bring them to the circle.*
This is a Quaker story about some of the wonderful ways of God's love. These ways are very important to Friends.	
	Lay down underlay and smooth it out.
In each person—in you and in me—there is a deep, deep place. It is a place where God is at home in us and where we are at home in God.	*At "deep, deep place," gently lay down the flame cutout in center of the underlay. Place one hand over it as in blessing, or lay a hand on it to "ground" it.*
God loves us, and never stops loving. Day and night, wherever we are, God is with us. And God is love.	*Take out heart-shaped visuals and place them on the underlay with the graphic side facing down and arranged in the following way:* - *"peace" at twelve o'clock from the perspective of the children (the edge closest to the storyteller)* - *"equality" at about two o'clock* - *"integrity" at four o'clock* - *"simplicity" at six o'clock* - *"community" at eight o'clock* - *"stewardship" at ten o'clock*
Love helps us be kind and gentle.	*Turn over heart at 12 o'clock to reveal the "peace" graphic.*
Love helps us be fair and welcoming to everyone.	*Turn over heart at two o'clock to reveal "equality" graphic.*
Love helps us be honest and true.	*Moving around the clock reveal "integrity" graphic.*
Love helps us know what is really important.	*Reveal "simplicity" graphic.*

Love helps everyone to be part of the group.	*Reveal "community" graphic.*
Love helps us to care for our earth.	*Reveal "stewardship" graphic.*
God's love helps us to live the ways of love. When we make mistakes, and even if we do something bad on purpose, God still loves us. Day by day, love reminds us of these six wonderful ways to live.	*Indicate flame at "love reminds us…"*
This child would not let her friend join a game. That made her friend cry. When she listened in her heart, she knew she had made a mistake. She invited her friend to play with her.	*Take child figure out of basket and hold it lovingly in your hand while talking about her, then place figure next to peace graphic on the flame side.*
This is the way of peace. It is love's way.	*On "this," indicate peace graphic with palms up, pause, and then on "love," indicate flame cutout with palm down.*
This child has friends who have dark skin and friends who have light skin. Some of his friends are big and some are little. Some are always kind, and some of them forget to be kind. He is friendly and fair with all of them.	*Take child figure out of basket and hold it lovingly in your hand while talking about him, then place figure next to equality graphic on the flame side.*
This is the way of equality. It is love's way.	*On "this," indicate equality graphic with palms up, pause, and then on "love," indicate flame cutout with palm down.*
This child lied to his mother. He didn't tell her the whole truth. Later he felt bad inside. He knew what he did was wrong. He then told his mother the whole truth.	*Take child figure out of basket and hold it lovingly in your hand while talking about him, then place figure next to integrity graphic on the flame side.*
This is the way of integrity. It is love's way.	*On "this," indicate integrity graphic with palms up, pause, and then on "love," indicate flame cutout with palm down.*
This child loves to play. Her day is *full* of play, with books and toys and games. At the end of the day, when she is tucked into bed, what is most important to her is the love she feels in her heart: the love of God, family and friends.	*Take child figure out of basket and hold it lovingly in your hand while talking about her, then place figure next to simplicity graphic on the flame side.*
This is the way of simplicity. It is love's way.	*On "this," indicate simplicity graphic with palms up, pause, and then on "love," indicate flame cutout with palm down.*

This child enjoys doing things with other people. Group projects and games are fun because everyone gets to feel part of the group. He is glad when everyone has a chance to join in.	*Take child figure out of basket and hold it in the palm of your hand while talking about him, then place figure next to community graphic on the flame side.*
This is the way of community. It is love's way.	*On "this," indicate community graphic with palms up, pause, and then on "love," indicate flame cutout with palm down.*
This child loves to be outside in nature. She watches things grow, listens to the wind blow, and feels the sun shine. Helping to take care of the earth makes her happy and hopeful.	*Take child figure out of basket and hold it in the palm of your hand while talking about her, then place figure next to stewardship graphic on the flame side.*
This is the way of stewardship. It is love's way.	*On "this," indicate stewardship graphic with palms up, pause, and then on "love," indicate flame cutout with palm down.*
God's love helps us to live the ways of love. When we make mistakes, and even if we do something bad on purpose, God still loves us. Day by day, love reminds us of these six wonderful ways to live:	*On "love reminds us," indicate the flame graphic.*
Being kind and gentle . . . Being fair and welcoming to everyone . . . Being honest and true . . . Knowing what is most important . . . Working well with others . . . Caring for the earth . . .	*Indicate each of the appropriate graphics as these as named. (They are described here in this order: peace, equality, integrity, simplicity, community, and stewardship.)*
	Pause. When you begin the wondering, look up at participants to indicate you welcome their responses.
I wonder what part of this story you like best.	*[You might not want to use all of these wonderings each time. Use your discernment, based on the developmental level of the individuals in the group and your sense of the movements of the Spirit.]*
I wonder what part is the most important to you today.	
I wonder where you have seen love.	
I wonder what the world would be like if everyone practiced the wonderful ways of God's love.	
I wonder what you might do today to live love's way.	
I wonder what you wonder about this story.	

Living the Ways of the Spirit
A story about testimonies drawing on the life of Jesus

Photo taken from perspective of the listeners.

Materials (graphics identical to those used in Love's Way)

- a circle of medium blue felt about 24" in diameter (the underlay)
- a single flame graphic about 3½–4" high made of successive layers of orange, yellow and red felt, with each of the three layers smaller than the previous one
- a red felt disk about 5½" in diameter (the flame is placed on top of the disk) (See templates for flame and circle in Appendices.)
- 5 wooden hearts, about 5" in diameter
- wooden graphics to glue onto each of the hearts to represent testimonies of simplicity, integrity, peace, equality, and community. Here are suggested graphics: a small heart (integrity), a person figure with arms extended and holding a small gold heart (simplicity), a dove cutout (peace), two people cutouts in different colors placed side by side (equality), and three to five flat people figures also in different colors and arranged in a circle (community).
- 5 wooden or heavy paper plaques, approximately 2 x 5 inches, each with a different testimony written on it: simplicity, integrity, peace, equality, community (as in the Faith & Play story, *Let Your Life Speak*)

Faith & Play™ | Living the Ways of the Spirit

WORDS	MOVEMENTS

[*Optional*: Watch where I go to get this story so you will always know where to find it. It's not where the sacred stories are. It's not where the parables are.]

Go to story materials and bring them to the circle.

This is a Quaker story about living the ways of the Spirit. Friends call these ways testimonies.

One place to begin is long ago with Jesus. The baby Jesus was born. He grew to be a child like you, and grew to be a man. We know about him today because the many wonderful things he said and did were from the power of God's Spirit within him.

Lay down underlay and smooth it out.

Place disk and flame cutout at center of underlay.

Jesus knew in his heart what is truly important. He did not own many things, and shared what he had. His heart was always open to God and to other people.

Take out simplicity graphic and hold it in the palm of one hand.

Jesus told people to be like children. The most important things are having the open heart, trust, and wonder of a young child.

Place graphic on underlay at 12 o'clock from the children's perspective.

We might call this simplicity.

Take simplicity plaque from basket and lay next to the simplicity graphic.

What Jesus said and did were from the power of the Spirit within him. This same Spirit is within us; when we listen and follow, the Spirit leads *us*, too.

With an open hand, indicate the flame cutout.

In Jesus' life and in his relationships, what he believed on the inside and his actions on the outside were one and the same. For example, he talked about love, but he didn't just talk; he lived love. He fed the hungry, visited the sick, and helped people.

Take out integrity graphic (heart) and rest it in the palm of one hand.

Because he was always honest and true, and because his words and actions were one, people knew they could trust him.

Place the graphic on underlay at 2 o'clock.

This is the way of integrity.

Place integrity plaque next to integrity graphic.

What Jesus said and did were from the power of the Spirit within him. This same Spirit is within us; when we listen and follow, the Spirit leads *us*, too.	*With an open hand, indicate the flame cutout.*
Jesus shared the good news of God's love for everyone. Some people did not like this message. They insulted and hit him, but he would not fight back. He chose patience, compassion, and wisdom. In his words and in his actions, he built greater understanding and justice.	*Take out peace graphic and rest it in the palm of one hand.*
	Place peace graphic on underlay between 4 and 5 o-clock.
This is the way of peace.	*Place peace plaque on underlay next to peace graphic.*
What Jesus said and did were from the power of the Spirit within him. This same Spirit is within us; when we listen and follow, this same Spirit leads *us*, too.	*With an open hand, indicate the flame cutout.*
Jesus said the love and power of God are in people's hearts. God welcomes everyone and loves everyone of every color, size, and shape, even when they do bad things. Jesus demonstrated God's welcome.	*Take out equality graphic and rest in the palm of one hand.*
In Jesus' day, just as today, there were people who were left out, people whom others wouldn't even talk to because they were different. But Jesus offered friendship to them all.	*Place the graphic on underlay at about 7 o'clock.*
This is the way of equality.	*Place equality plaque on underlay next to graphic.*
What Jesus said and did were from the power of the Spirit within him. This same Spirit is within us; when we listen and follow, this same Spirit leads *us*, too.	*With an open hand, indicate the flame cutout.*
Jesus welcomed as his friends and followers many different kinds of people.	*Take out community graphic and rest in the palm of one hand.*
They worked together for peace and justice. They supported and helped one another with care, respect and love. They were like a family.	*Place the graphic on underlay at 10 o'clock.*
This is community.	*Place community plaque on underlay next to community graphic.*

What Jesus said and did were from the power of the Spirit within him. This same Spirit is within us, and when we listen and follow, the Spirit leads *us*, too.	*With an open hand, indicate the flame cutout.*
The Spirit that worked with amazing power in Jesus is in us today. Friends testify that wherever the Spirit is listened to and followed, there is simplicity, integrity, peace, equality, and community.	*Indicate visuals for each testimony as it is named.*
We sometimes call the wonderful ways of the Spirit *testimonies*. This is because they testify to, or show, the work of the Spirit within us. When we listen and follow, the Spirit leads us in these ways.	*Indicate, with an open hand, the flame cutout in center of underlay.*
	Pause. When you begin the wondering, look up at participants to indicate you welcome their responses.
I wonder what part of this story you like best.	*[You will probably not want to use all of these wonderings, at least not each time. Use your discernment, based on the developmental level of the individuals in the group and your sense of the movements of the Spirit.]*
I wonder what part is the most important to you today.	
I wonder where you are in the story, or what part is about you.	
I wonder if there is any part of the story we could leave out and still have all the story we need.	
I wonder if there is anything in this room that you might place here to remind us of any of these ways.	*Have children select and place objects on the underlay to represent various testimonies.*
I wonder what the world would be like if everyone listened to and followed the Spirit.	
I wonder what things we might do today (or this week) to live in the ways of the Spirit.	
I wonder if the Spirit might be as powerful in our meeting community as it was in Jesus' life.	
I wonder what you wonder about this story.	

Let Your Life Speak

A story for older children about the testimonies and what happens when we live our lives guided by Spirit

Photo taken from perspective of the listeners.

Materials

○ Medium blue felt underlay, 24" square.

○ Small red felt circle about 5½" in diameter.

○ Six people figures varying in size, shape and color, with a red dot or oval painted on each.

○ Length of red yarn about 45" long.

○ Two-dimensional figures of a heart (gold, 2½"), a dove (white, 4") and a disc painted to resemble the earth (blue, green and white, 3")

○ A set of 3 nesting dolls, also called matryoshka (3½" tall), painted per photo. If you cannot find nesting dolls, see note at end of story.

○ Six rectangular plaques with the name of a testimony written on each, and the first letter of that testimony on the reverse side.

WORDS	MOVEMENTS
[*Optional:* Watch where I go to get this story so you will always know where to find it. It's not where the sacred stories are. It's not where the parables are.]	*Get story materials from the Quaker story area and return to your place in the circle.*
This is a Quaker story about Friends' testimonies, and what happens when we live our lives guided by Spirit.	*Open underlay.*
We know there is a deep, deep place where we are at home in God and God is at home in us.	
We know that Spirit is always near us, as close as breath. When we stop and listen, we know deep down what is true. We know how to love, what to do, who to be.	*Set out red circle, and touch gently.*
When Friends are guided by that still small voice within, Spirit consistently leads us to equality, community, peace, integrity, simplicity and stewardship. Quakers call these *testimonies*. In living them out in an everyday world, our lives become testament to what is good and whole and true.	*As you name the testimonies, set out plaques with name of each at front edge of underlay.*
How we treat one another, what we do, the way we dress, how we speak, all testify to how Spirit is working within us.	
When we listen, deep down, we know that God loves each and every one of us. We know there is a spark of the Divine in all of us. This is the basis for the EQUALITY testimony. Female and male, rich and poor, old and young, brave and not so brave, people of all colors, God loves us all.	*As you speak, tenderly show a people figure, indicating red dot as "spark of Divine." Set out figures in a circle, then point to various ones as "female and male, rich and poor" etc.*
And because God loves us, we are called to love one another. We try to see the goodness in everyone, even when that is hard. We treat all people with respect.	
Our actions testify to our belief that there is "that of God" in everyone.	
Spirit shows the way.	*Indicate red circle.*

When we listen, deep down, we know that because God loves us all equally, as parents love their children, we are all related to one another as brothers and sisters in the great family of humanity.

God calls us to live together in peace, with respect and affection; to care for one another and make decisions for the good of all. We call this COMMUNITY. In our relationships to others, we practice how to love, what to do, who to be.

Form a circle of red yarn around the people figures.

Spirit shows the way.

Indicate red circle.

When we listen, deep down, and know there is "that of God" in every person, we realize it is not right to injure another person in any way, even when we disagree. The PEACE testimony begins with refusing to harm another person.

Place peace dove in circle.

It also means choosing to work actively for peace.

- This one works to remove causes of conflict.
- This one teaches peaceful means of resolving disputes.
- Another advocates for peace and participates in protests.
- This one finds ways to help those harmed by war.
- This one works for racial justice.

Indicate various figures representing people who promote peace.

There are many ways to nurture peace.

Spirit shows the way.

Indicate red circle.

When we listen, deep down, we know what is right. Sometimes what is right can be hidden and hard to discern. At other times, what is right may be clear, but following through may be, for some reason, difficult. When Friends both listen for what is right *and* live in ways that reflect that truth, they are showing INTEGRITY.

The word integrity means whole, complete, undivided, and that's the way it feels when we live with integrity.	*Place gold heart within circle of people figures.*
Integrity means that what a person believes on the inside, and how they act on the outside, are one and the same.	*Turn heart over to show other side.*
Spirit shows the way.	*Indicate red circle.*
When we listen, deep down, we know what is important. Our lives are full of choices. It can be confusing. How many activities we try to do, what we choose to buy, own, and consume. In Meeting for Worship, we try to use as few words as possible, yet as many as are needed.	*Pick up nesting dolls; look at outside one as you speak.*
God calls us to discern the difference between what is essential and what we can choose to do without. We call this SIMPLICITY.	*Open second doll, comparing it to first.*
We need to continually clear away whatever is not really necessary, to make it easier to focus on what is *truly important*.	*Show smallest doll at "genuinely important," then place it in the circle.*

Many of us have found we are happier when our lives are less crowded: less is often more.

Spirit shows the way. *Indicate red circle.*

When we listen, deep down, we know that everything—all we have, the world we live in—is a gift from God. The testimony of STEWARDSHIP recognizes that we are caretakers, not owners, of the earth.

Use hands to make protective gesture around props, then set out "earth" disk.

Spirit guides us to walk gently and provide for the future. It means protecting our forests and our waters. It means caring for our buildings and other goods so they last. It could mean recycling, and choosing a fuel-efficient car and appliances.

Our goal is to care for things with love and respect, so they will last, and not be lost or wasted. Spirit shows the way.

Indicate red circle.

These six testimonies are the ones Friends today generally recognize as the most important. Many people use the first letters of each of these words to help us remember them all. S-P-I-C-E-S, spices.

Make clockwise gesture around props.

Then turn over each plaque, arranging them so they spell "spices."

The testimonies are not a set of rules to be memorized. They are a reflection of how we live when led by Spirit. They are what Quakers mean when we say, "Let your life speak." Actions speak louder than words: they are testament to our beliefs, an indication of who we really are.

Sit back and reflect silently on the testimonies.

When we listen to God, and are led by Spirit, we know how to love, what to do, who to be. Our lives become whole and holy. Perhaps we begin to live that Kingdom of Heaven that Jesus spoke of, right here on earth.

Touch red "Spirit" circle.

Pause. When you begin the wondering, look up at participants to indicate you welcome their responses.

Faith & Play™ | Let Your Life Speak

I wonder which testimonies speak to you today.

I wonder which you find most challenging. I wonder what helps you stop and listen to the voice of Spirit.

I wonder if there is a testimony we could leave out and still have all we need.

I wonder if/how the testimonies are related to one another.

I wonder what ways you can think of to live the (fill in blank) testimony.

I wonder what would happen if more and more people lived led by Spirit.

I wonder what our lives are saying about us.

Note to storytellers:

- Older students might also be engaged in wondering around **"Who** have let their lives speak?" Who are Friends or other leaders who live the Quaker testimonies in their witness and work?
- When the story is told to middle school-age youth, the lesson might be extended with a discussion about the historical provenance of Friends testimonies (e.g. the 1660 peace testimony sent to the English king by early Friends including George Fox, and the relatively modern emphasis on stewardship).
- Unpainted, blank sets of three nesting dolls can be found online at sites like "Best Pysanky" or Etsy.
- Another way of making the materials for the testimony of simplicity is to make three cut-out figures of the same shape (flat, gingerbread-like people) in three sizes. Decorate like the matryoshka dolls, but stack them (largest, busiest design on top) and reveal each simpler piece underneath in the same way you would "unpack" the dolls.

Stories of Witness

George Fox's Big Discovery

A story about a way God reveals Truth to us

Photo taken from perspective of the listeners.

Materials

- Square tan or light brown felt underlay, 24" square.
- A simple George Fox figure about 4" or 5" high. Optional: Assorted people figures, of different shapes and sizes, to use at the end of the story to represent Friends today.
- Four plaques, about 6" x 6" with the following four graphics glued or painted on them: a church, a book, a sword, and music notes. One corner of each card should be cut so that when placed side by side the cut-outs form the shape of a heart the same size as your heart cutout. The cuts should be made in the following places: the bottom right corner of the church card, the bottom left corner of the book card, the top right corner of the sword card, and the top left corner of the music card. Each cut creates one quarter of a heart shape. See photo and templates.
- One red heart shape, felt or wood, the same size as the space created by the four plaques, about 4" at widest point.

WORDS	MOVEMENTS
[*Optional*: Watch where I go to get this story so you will always know where to find it. It's not where the sacred stories are. It's not where the parables are.]	*Get story materials and return to your place in the circle. Put story materials beside you*
This is a Quaker story about George Fox's big discovery.	*Spread out underlay and smooth it out.*
George Fox lived in England long ago. When he was a child, he went to church and he read the Bible. He learned things about God. When he got older, he wanted to know more. He had many questions about God, about life, about love.	*Place George Fox figure on underlay on the side closest to the children.*
The questions in his heart were very big. He looked everywhere, but no one could answer them for him. The questions were very heavy. It was hard for him to carry them around.	*Slowly move figure around the underlay, pausing from time to time.*
George Fox looked for answers in church. There were many people there, but no one could answer his big questions. (pause)	*Place piece with church graphic at near right corner of underlay. Move figure over to the image, pause, then move figure either to side closest to children or to storyteller.*
He read books. But the answers to his big, heavy questions were not in them. (pause)	*Place piece with book graphic at near left corner of underlay. Move figure over to the image, pause, then move figure either to side closest to children or to storyteller.*
George Fox could not rest. He worried. He prayed. Some people said, "Forget about your questions, George. Why don't you become a soldier?" But he didn't want to fight. Besides, he was looking for answers, not a different job. (*Pause.*)	*Place piece with sword graphic at far right corner of underlay. Move figure over to the image, pause, then move figure either to side closest to children or to storyteller.*
He searched some more. He walked and walked. Some people said, "Don't worry, George. Sing hymns with us." But George Fox didn't feel like singing. He only wanted answers. (*Pause.*)	*Place piece with music notation at far left corner of underlay. Move figure over to the image, pause, then move figure either to side closest to children or to storyteller.*

He looked for a very long time. Finally, he did find one who could answer his big, heavy questions! Do you know who that was? George Fox discovered that in his heart God was whispering little pieces of the answers the whole time—just as much as he was ready to understand.

[*Optional*: Fox wrote in his journal: "I heard a voice which said, "There is one, even Christ Jesus, that can speak to thy condition; and when I heard it my heart did leap for joy.]

From then on George Fox knew he had pieces of the answers in his heart wherever he was, because God was always with him. God was whispering in his heart …

Place heart at center of underlay. Move figure close to the heart shape. Cup hand over heart.

when he was in a church building … (*Pause.*)

Put piece with church graphic next to heart. (Note each piece has a cut out corner to fit the shape of one quarter of the heart.)

when he was reading … (*Pause.*)

Put piece with book graphic next to heart.

when people were fighting … (*Pause.*)

Put piece with sword graphic next to heart.

when everyone was singing … (*Pause.*)

Put piece with music notes next to heart.

He learned to listen hard because God is sometimes *hidden* inside. God's voice can be very still and small. (*Pause.*)

Place your open hand with fingers spread over the heart.

George Fox realized there are some questions that only God can answer. And if we stop and listen, we will find that God is already giving us the answers, just as many as we are ready to understand.

George was so happy that he shared his discovery with other people. Many of those people joined with him. They listened and prayed together. They called themselves Friends. And we call ourselves Friends.

As you affirm our being Friends today, set out additional people figures next to George Fox. You might also pass around a basket of people figures for listeners to add a Friend to the story.

Faith & Play™ | George Fox's Big Discovery

Pause. When you begin the wondering, look up at participants to indicate you welcome their responses.

I wonder what part of this story you like best.

I wonder what part of the story is the most important to you right now.

I wonder where you are in the story or what part of the story is about you.

I wonder what you wonder about this story.

I wonder if you know someone like this.

Sources

This story is based on the opening chapter of George Fox's *Journal* and was initially inspired by a George Fox story by Mary Snyder in her resource, *Quakers I and II*, published by Quaker Cottage Industries, 2002.

Faith & Play™ | George Fox's Big Discovery 73

Margaret Fell of Swarthmoor Hall

An early Friend gives Quakerism a home

Photo taken from perspective of the listeners.

Materials

- English meadow green (medium green) felt underlay cut in oval or rectangular shape; approximately 28" x 24".
- People figures for Margaret Fell and George Fox. Margaret Fell figure can wear a red shawl.
- Gray felt house with flat roof and pitched sides (Swarthmoor Hall); 9" x 12".
- Darker gray felt shapes to define roof and represent 4–5 windows and doorway (see photo of house at end of story).
- Felt shapes of heart, flame, and "stones" for path.
- Small box to hold felt "stones" for path in front of house.
- Prison door with barred window cut out (black or dark brown stiff felt).

- Documents for letter and "Women's Speaking Justified" mounted on card stock or stiff felt. The latter is provided at end of this document. For the letter, you can hand write a small version using parchment and black ink, or use the optional feather "quill pen" to represent the letter in the story.
- Optional: Feather "quill pen".

WORDS	MOVEMENTS
[*Optional:* Watch where I go to get this story so you will always know where to find it. It's not where the sacred stories are. It's not where the parables are.]	*Get story materials from the Quaker story area and return to your place in the circle. Put story materials beside you.*
This is a story of Quaker faith and witness. It is about someone who listened to the still, small voice within and discovered what God wanted her to do. Her beliefs on the inside and her actions on the outside became one and the same. Her actions bore witness to Truth.	*Hold one hand palm up for "inside," other palm up for "outside." Bring palms together in prayer position for "same."*
Margaret Fell lived in England at the same time as George Fox, the founder of Quakerism.	*Smooth out green felt underlay, with the oval longer left to right.* *Place Margaret Fell on underlay, on the bottom left side from your perspective.*
She lived in a big house called Swarthmoor Hall with her family.	*Lay gray felt in the shape of a building (Swarthmoor Hall) on top of green underlay. Place roof, door and windows (if not glued) on house. Take your time.*
Her heart was here, with her husband and seven children and the work of caring for her family. It was a home filled with love.	*Place felt heart on the left side of the house (storyteller's right).*
Margaret had the gift of welcome. Visitors and travelers stopped at Swarthmoor Hall for a meal and a place to stay the night.	*Indicate doorway of Swarthmoor Hall.*
Some of the travelers shared ideas about God and faith. Some ideas were different from what she heard in church. Margaret had many questions; she listened carefully for a message that would speak to her heart and answer her questions.	

Faith & Play™ | Margaret Fell of Swarthmoor Hall

One day Margaret Fell heard a traveler named George Fox preach. He spoke his message of the Light within; that each person can listen for God.	*Place Fox figure at the bottom of the underlay, across from Fell on other side of the doorway.*
Fox asked, "What canst thou say?" When you listen to the Light within you, what can you say about God?	*Place the flame on the right side of Swarthmoor Hall (storyteller's left). Indicate flame again when say, "Light."*
When she heard these words, Margaret realized that she and other people did not speak truth from their hearts, and were not listening for God and to the Light within. Instead, they took their truth from other places.	*Cup your hand around Fell, to indicate that she is speaking.*
"We are all thieves!" she cried.	
Fox's words opened Margaret Fell's heart. She had been seeking an answer, but a question had been the answer.	
	Pause a moment to reflect on her opening. Place Fox figure back into basket.
Margaret began to worship in silence, in her home, listening for God to speak to her and to find Truth for herself.	*Move Fell in front of door on green underlay.*
She listened to the Light within, and asked, what can I say?	*Indicate the flame.*
She could say, "Welcome." And so she did.	
	Lay your hand like a blessing on the gray house.
Swarthmoor Hall became a haven, a safe place for Quakers. It was a home where they could worship together to listen for God.	*Indicate the flame.*
When she was arrested for allowing meeting for worship at Swarthmoor Hall, Margaret Fell listened to the Spirit, and asked, what can I say?	
	Move Margaret Fell in front of the flame on the underlay.
She said that as long as God blessed her with a home, she would worship in it.	
Margaret went to Prison	*Place "prison bars" cut out in front of her on the underlay (standing in front of her). Optional: place small feather (quill pen) in front of the prison bars.*

While she was there, she wrote to other Quakers. She listened for Truth, and asked, "What can I say?" She spoke through her many letters to Friends, and encouraged them.

She spoke through the pamphlets she wrote that many people read. She said that women have the Light within them and that women can speak Truth. Women can speak from their hearts in worship, and in meeting for business. Because of her voice, people are equal partners in a Quaker wedding ceremony.

Margaret was released from prison. She came home. Margaret listened for God, and asked, "What can I say? What can I do?"

Margaret spoke through her actions.

She took care of her family.

She helped Quakers who were in jail, and their families.

She supported new meetings and started Women's Business Meetings to take care of poor and hungry people, Quaker and not Quaker.

She travelled to speak before kings, telling them of the Quakers' faith and message of peace.

But all the paths she followed always led her home, to Swarthmoor Hall. She welcomed Friends and visitors there throughout her long life.

Margaret Fell is sometimes called the "Mother of Quakerism." She was asked, "What can you say?" and she answered with a life that spoke.

I wonder what part of the story you like best.

Place small letter in front of underlay.

Place small document ("Women's Speaking Justified") next to letter.

Cup your hand over Margaret.

Remove prison bars; place back in basket.

Lay out stones in path along bottom of green underlay, leading from doorway to front edge of underlay. Lay them out one by one as you name parts of her work. Have Fell walk out with them.

Move Fell back along stone path to the house.

Cup your hand around Fell.

Pause. When you begin the wondering, look up at participants to indicate you welcome their responses.

I wonder what part of the story is most important to you, today.

I wonder where you are in the story, or what part feels like it is about you.

I wonder when you have heard your voice speak Truth? I wonder what you can say about it.

I wonder when you have shared your gift of welcome? I wonder where is a special place you come back to again and again.

I wonder if you know someone like this.   *Indicate Margaret Fell.*

I wonder if there is any part of the story we could take out, and still have all the story we need.

Note to storytellers:

This story focuses on Margaret Fell, how she opened her heart and home to the Quaker faith, and her contributions to the community's early survival. While it is not directly mentioned that George Fox was her (second) husband, consider how to share this connection with children hearing the story. One option is to first tell "George Fox's Big Discovery," and then share the Fell story as a "side by side." If you choose to add a red shawl to the Margaret Fell figure in this story, and are asked about it, red was a popular color during that period, and we have evidence that George Fox bought red fabric for Margaret to make "a mantle."

Children may wonder why Fell and other Friends were imprisoned for their religious beliefs. Language based on 'Mary Fisher Carries the Quaker Message Near and Far" might be helpful here: "Friends spoke out about the power of God in each person that could change the world. But at that time, some people were afraid of this message and put Friends in prison. These were difficult places, but the Friends there lived in God's love, power and light, so they knew God's peace. Quakers worshipped and prayed together. They sang together. They helped one another."

If you chose to extend the story experience with First Day School lessons, there is a Philadelphia Yearly Meeting curriculum that includes a chapter on Margaret Fell, and can be downloaded for free from:
www.pym.org/publications/files/2013/01/yc20-fc-Quakers-Answer-the-Call.pdf

Timeline of Margaret Fell's life:

- **1614** Margaret Askew born. Upon her father's death she inherits £6000 (approximately £975,600 in 2013).
- **1632** Marries Thomas Fell; they have nine children together, eight survive to adulthood.
- **June 1652** George Fox visits Swarthmoor Hall.
- **1652-1658** Swarthmoor Hall becomes a center of Quaker activity.
- **1658** Judge Thomas Fell dies; Margaret inherits Swarthmoor Hall, which remained a meeting place and haven from persecution. Her son George Fell (age 20) inherited control of the rest of the estate. The trustees are Anthony Pearson and Gervase Benson, both Friends.
- **1660-1698** Margaret Fell makes 10 journeys in these years between her home in the north of England to London in the south where she lobbies the king and court on behalf of Friends, and ministers to the needs of meetings.
- **1664-1668** Margaret Fell is arrested for failing to take an oath and for allowing Quaker Meetings to be held in her home. She is sentenced to life imprisonment and forfeiture of her property. During this time she writes *Women's Speaking Justified, Proved and Allowed of by the Scriptures, All Such as Speak by the Spirit and Power of the Lord Jesus And How Women Were the First That Preached the Tidings of the Resurrection of Jesus, and Were Sent by Christ's Own Command Before He Ascended to the Father* (John 20:17) among other works.
- **January 1665** The King grants Margaret's forfeited estate to her son George Fell, who was no longer a Quaker. However, he left his sisters in charge of Swarthmoor Hall, and Quaker meetings continued there unabated.
- **1668** Margaret is released by order of the King and council.
- **1669** Margaret Fell and George Fox marry, after obtaining clearness from her children and Friends in Bristol.
- **1670-1671** Margaret endures another prison sentence.
- **1688** Meetinghouse built at Swarthmoor Hall.
- **1689** James II issues the act of Toleration and all Quakers are freed from prison.
- **1691** George Fox dies at age 67.
- **1702** Margaret Fell dies at age 88.

Swarthmoor Hall, Ulverston, Cumbria, United Kingdom

As seen in photo of story materials, reproduce this 2″ x 2½″ image, cut out, and mount on light cardboard.

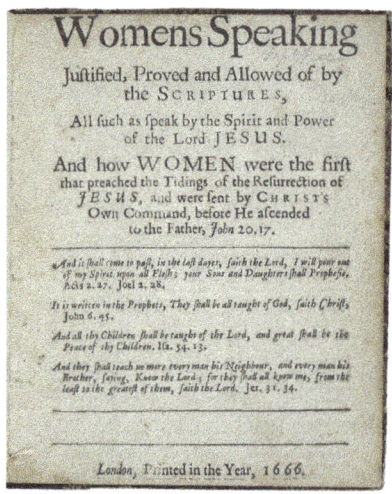

80   Faith & Play™ | Margaret Fell of Swarthmoor Hall

Mary Fisher Carries the Quaker Message Near and Far

A story about an early Friend who lived in God's love, power, and peace

Photo taken from perspective of the listeners.

Materials

- A medium blue underlay, roughly 18" x 36" to represent the ocean.
- Three felt "islands" to represent Turkey (6" x 9" in light brown or tan), North American colonies (6" x 9" in dark green), and England (5" x 8" in meadow green)
- Four free standing figures: one Quaker woman, one ornate Turkish sultan, and two Turkish "attendants." (See information on making people and clothing in Appendices.)
- A small piece of fabric with a pattern similar to an oriental carpet.
- A small boat large enough to support Mary's figure (for safety reasons, avoid having a mast if working with young children).
- A cut-out of a jail made of stiff felt with a barred window so that Mary Fisher's head is visible when the jail is placed in front of her.

WORDS

[*Optional*: Watch where I go to get this story so you will always know where to find it. It's not where the sacred stories are. It's not where the parables are.]

MOVEMENTS

Get story materials and return to your place in the circle. Put materials beside you.

This is a story of Quaker faith and witness. It is about someone who listened to the still, small voice within and discovered what God wanted her to do. Her beliefs on the inside and her actions on the outside became one and the same. Her actions bore witness to Truth.	*Get out the underlay and smooth it out. Then lay down the three "islands" to represent (from storyteller's right to left) the American colonies, England, and Turkey.*
Mary Fisher lived in England long ago, the same time as George Fox. She was poor and could not read or write. She worked as a servant for a rich family.	*Take the Mary Fisher figure out of the basket and place it on the piece of felt representing England.*
One day she heard some Quakers preach about God's love, power and light. Through the words and actions of the Quakers, she discovered the power of God within herself. She became a Friend. She spoke out about the power of God in each person that could change the world.	
But some people were afraid of her message and put her in jail.	*Place jail door in front of the Mary Fisher figure.*
Mary was not the only Quaker there. She and the other Quakers worshipped and prayed together. They sang together. The Quakers helped Mary. They taught her how to read and write. The jail was a very difficult place, but they lived in God's love, power and light, so they knew God's peace.	*Cup a hand over the jail in blessing.*
Finally, Mary got out of jail.	*Remove jail door and return it to basket.*
Mary felt God ask her to go to America to tell people about God's love, power and peace. She crossed the Atlantic Ocean.	*Move ship across "water" toward felt "island" on your right. Take your time moving the boat for each voyage in the story. The movements across the water can represent the difficulty of the journey, like the desert crossings in some Godly Play stories.*
The ship finally arrived in Boston, a place where there was not one Quaker.	*Rest the boat and figure at the American colonies felt island.*
When Mary got off the ship, she was sent straight to jail.	*Remove the Mary figure from boat and place jail in front of her.*

The governor there was afraid of her message of God's love, power and peace. He burned all her books. He was so afraid of Mary Fisher that he boarded up the jail window so no one could see or hear her.	*Place your hand over the window of the jail.*
After a month, the governor put her on a ship and sent her away.	*Place figure on ship and move across the blue to England.*
Back in England, Mary felt God ask her to go to the place now called Turkey to talk to their leader, called a sultan. In those days, people in England believed the Turkish people wanted only violence and war, and were afraid of them. Mary wanted to tell the sultan about God's love, power, and peace.	*Lay hand on felt island to indicate Turkey.*
It was a long, difficult journey, but God was with her to help her.	*Place Mary figure on ship and begin moving toward Turkey (to your left).*
[*Optional text for older children:* When she got very close to Turkey, an English officer told her it was too dangerous for a woman to go to Turkey. He put her on another ship and told the captain to take her back to England. Mary did not fight. She calmly got on the new ship and started back.	*[For older children: Stop ship near Turkey. Change direction of the ship, moving it a very short distance toward England.*
But Mary knew what she had to do. She convinced the ship's captain that she was neither silly nor crazy. The captain let her off at the next port. Mary was now over 500 miles away from Turkey. We don't know how she got to Turkey, but God was with her to help her.]	*Stop ship, take Mary out and hold her in one hand. With other hand return ship to the basket, or to England. Continue holding Mary figure in your hand.]*
Mary finally reached Turkey, but she had to search for the sultan. She asked many people for help, but no one would guide her. They were afraid of the power of the sultan. They thought they would be punished if the sultan did not want to see Mary Fisher.	*If skipping the bracketed words, stop ship at edge of Turkey and put it away. Take out Mary figure and hold it.*
We don't know how, but somehow she discovered where the sultan was. He was camped with 20,000 soldiers.	*Place Mary Fisher on edge of felt piece representing Turkey.*

Faith & Play™ | Mary Fisher Carries the Quaker Message Near and Far

The young sultan was in a silk tent embroidered in gold. Everyone was in their finest clothes, because they had heard Mary had a message from God, whom the people there called Allah.

Place carpet on Turkey, then add the sultan (in the center) with an attendant on either side. Figures should face the children.

Mary stood before the sultan in her simple gray dress and bonnet. She stood in silence. The sultan kindly invited her to speak, but Mary remained silent. The sultan waited. Mary was waiting, too. She knew God would give her the words to speak out of the silence.

Place Mary on carpet, facing the sultan.

> The light of God shines in each person.
> In this light is love.
> In this light is truth.
> In this light is power.
> In this light is peace.

The sultan listened and said "You have spoken the truth." Mary had done what God had asked her to do.

Mary returned to England.

Place Mary on ship and move ship to England.

We will remember her as the brave Quaker woman who shared the good news of God's love, power, and peace.

Pause. When you begin the wondering, look up at participants to indicate you welcome their responses.

I wonder what part of this story you like best.

I wonder what part is most important for you today.

I wonder where you are in the story, or what part of the story is about you.

I wonder if there is any part we could leave out and still have all the story we need.

I wonder if you have ever waited in silence for God.

When wondering with older children or in multigenerational settings, you may want to ask the following "wonderings."

I wonder how Mary knew it was God who was asking her to do such amazing things.

I wonder if you have ever felt led to do something that was very difficult or unpopular.

I wonder if you know someone like this.

Notes for storytellers:

Mary Fisher (1623–98) was a Quaker missionary, one of the "Valiant Sixty" who were responsible for the early, explosive growth of the Religious Society of Friends. Traveling in the company of Ann Austin, she reached Boston in July, 1656, where the Puritans in power rejected her message forcefully, as shown in the story.

Mary Fisher was probably not the first Quaker to reach North America. Another woman, Elizabeth Harris, reached Virginia and Maryland possibly in late 1655, certainly by 1656. She was received in a far more positive way by Puritans in power there, among whom "many convincements were made," principally in the Annapolis and Kent Island, Maryland area.

The trip to Turkey took place in 1658. The sultan's name was Mohammed (or Mahomet) IV. Although he was only 17 years old, he was very powerful.

In later life, Mary Fisher married first William Bayley, with whom she had three children, then after his death John Crosse. With Crosse and her children she emigrated to Charleston, South Carolina, where she lived for the rest of her life. She is buried there.

Sources

Lighting Candles in the Dark: Stories of Courage and Love in Action, Quaker Press of FGC, 2001 reprint

Unbridled Spirits: Women of the English Revolution: 1640-1660, Stevie Davies, The Women's Press Ltd, 1998. Photo taken from perspective of the children.

Historical Dictionary of the Friends (Quakers), Abbott, Chijioke, Dandelion, and Oliver

The Beginnings of Quakerism, William C. Braithwaite, William Sessions Limited, 1981

John Woolman, Gentle Abolitionist
A Friend acts to end slaveholding by Quakers

Photo taken from perspective of the listeners.

Materials

- Dark or forest green felt underlay 24" square.
- 7 European-American Quaker figures, 5 male and 2 female, in varying sizes and dressed in various shades of grey and other dark colors.
- 3 African-American figures, at least one female.
- An extra man's hat, off-white color; off-white felt "suit" with hook-and-loop (Velcro) or snap closures to wrap around grey Woolman figure. (John Woolman starts off as a grey-clad figure like the rest, and eventually changes into undyed hat and suit.)
- 3" wood heart, painted gold on both sides, with flame icon on one side (the "inside").
- Tan felt rectangle for store, 3" x 4". Items for store: at minimum, a barrel of molasses, bag of sugar, 3 bolts of dark cloth and one bolt of light cloth. Other items such as bucket, shovel, rake, washboard as desired.
- Several small printed items: a single sheet with word "Will" handwritten; and a printed essay, "On the Keeping of Negroes." (Provided at end of this document.)

Documents are provided at the end of this document, and will need to be reduced for the story materials.

Placement of materials during story:

Be sure to leave space between Quaker figures so you can reach the heart and turn it over without knocking down any figures each time you say the refrain "inside . . . and outside." Also, left-handed storytellers might find it works better to reverse placement of "store" and the documents so the store is to their left and easier to work with.

WORDS	MOVEMENTS
[*Optional*: Watch where I go to get this story so you will always know where to find it. It's not where the sacred stories are. It's not where the parables are.]	*Get story materials from the Quaker story area and return to your place in the circle. Put story materials beside you.*
This is a story of Quaker faith and witness. It is about someone who listened to the still, small voice within and discovered what God wanted him to do. His beliefs on the inside and his actions on the outside became one and the same. His actions bore witness to Truth.	*Hold one hand palm up for "inside," other palm up for "outside." Bring palms together in prayer position for "same."*
This is a story about John Woolman, a man who acted to end slavery among Friends.	*Smooth out underlay.*
John Woolman was born on a farm in a colony that is now called New Jersey.	*Gently hold Woolman figure; set on underlay near center.*
The people John saw every day were mainly other Quakers: his family, neighbors, school friends, members of his monthly meeting, his quarterly meeting, his yearly meeting in Philadelphia. All wore plain clothing made in quiet colors like grey. Some of it was dark, some lighter, some of fine fabric and some rough, but all wore the plain clothing chosen not bring attention to the individual. John was no different.	*Set out additional figures as you name each group.* *Indicate various shades of grey the figures are "wearing."* *Touch Woolman gently.*
From childhood, John Woolman tried to live in ways of the Spirit, guided by Truth. He believed deeply that, because there is That of God in every person, God loves all people equally. Thus we are called to treat all people with equal respect.	*Set out gold heart in front of Woolman.*

It was very important to him that what he believed on the inside, and how he acted on the outside, were one and the same.	*Show each side as you say "inside" and "outside." Leave "inside" facing up.*
In those days, there were people held as slaves in the American colonies. They had been stolen from their homes in Africa and brought across the ocean in chains. Today sometimes people think slavery happened only in the South; however, there were slaves in all the American colonies. There were Friends who held slaves, too.	*Gesture to include whole underlay. Set out 3 slave figures on various parts of underlay among the Friends.*
	Gesture to slave figures.
People who are slaves have to do what the master says. They have to live where the master says. They have to get up when the master says. They have to go to bed when the master says. They have to eat what the master says. They have to do the work the master says.	
	Pause briefly.
They have to do everything the master says. These freedoms were taken from them.	
John saw early on that slavery is wrong. Deep down, he knew holding people as slaves is not in keeping with God's love for all people.	*Indicate Woolman figure, then flame at "deep down."*
One day when John was at work, his boss told him to write a bill of sale for a slave woman named Sarah, whom John knew. Although he was uncomfortable about it, he wrote the bill of sale as told. Then his heart was filled with remorse. He knew deep down it is not right to sell a person as if they were an object instead of a human being. What he believed on the inside and how he acted on the outside were *not* the same.	*Move female slave figure from crowd next to John.*
	Cover heart icon with your hand, hiding it.
From that day on, it became his life's work to persuade Friends to free their slaves, and free themselves from the burden of slavery.	
He refused to write any papers related to buying or selling a slave, except if the papers would free the person.	*Set out "will" in lower left corner of underlay.*

He began to speak out against slavery wherever he went. John traveled far and wide over the years. He spoke respectfully to all, including to slaveholders. Perhaps because he spoke gently and listened carefully, slaveholders listened to him. Many did free their slaves.	*Move Woolman around underlay to "speak" to other Friends, returning to corner with "will."*
He also helped to write many essays which caused Friends to think about and talk about whether it is right to enslave another person.	*Set out "essay" next to "will."*
By doing these things, what he believed on the inside, and how he acted on the outside, became one and the same.	*Pick up gold heart, showing each side as you say "inside" and "outside."*
For much of his life, John Woolman was a shopkeeper and a tailor. In his store were many goods for keeping a home, tending a garden, feeding a family, clothing a family.	*Set out store with goods related to home, garden, etc. in lower right corner. Move Woolman to store.*
In time, he came to see that some things in his store, including food such as sugar and molasses, were made by slaves. He realized that if he bought or sold anything made by slave labor, he was in fact supporting slavery. So he stopped using sugar and molasses, and stopped selling them in his store.	*Point to each.* *Remove sugar and molasses.*
By doing this, what he believed on the inside, and how he acted on the outside, became one and the same.	*Pick up gold heart, showing each side as you say "inside" and "outside."*
There was one thing made by slave labor that was very hard for John to give up: the plain dark fabric for his clothing. The dyes used to make dark-colored fabric came from big farms called plantations, where slaves grew indigo plants.	*Indicate his dark clothing. Show 3 different bolts of dark cloth in one palm...*
Un-dyed fabric looked very different. If a person wore clothing made from un-dyed cloth, it would show they did not want to use anything made by slave labor. But it would also make them look very different from their friends, their family, their whole community.	*...next to a bolt of un-dyed cloth in other palm.* *Return fabric to store.*

Faith & Play™ | John Woolman, Gentle Abolitionist

The idea of looking different was hard for John to accept. He wrestled with the question of giving up dyed cloth for a long time, and prayed to find a way out of doing this. In the end, it became clear to him that to keep his integrity he would have to stop using dyed cloth, no matter how uncomfortable it made him.	*At "integrity" point to gold heart.*
He made the change one step at a time, as his clothing wore out. First, the hat.	*Take your time for each step. Remove grey hat; put it away. Show un-dyed hat, put it on.*
Then, his trousers wore out, and his jacket. So he replaced them with new ones made of un-dyed cloth.	*Re-clothe Woolman in light felt. Hold up figure. Then place him in middle of underlay, near heart.*
The un-dyed clothing indeed made John Woolman look different from everyone else. Yet he continued to dress in un-dyed cloth for the rest of his life.	
By doing this, what he believed on the inside, and how he acted on the outside, became one and the same.	*Pick up gold heart, showing each side as you say "inside" and "outside."*
At the urging of John Woolman and others, Quakers moved one step at a time to end slavery among Friends. First, Friends said no more *bringing* people from other countries as slaves. Next, no *buying or selling* people as slaves. And finally, no more *holding* people as slaves.	*At each step, move a slave figure and a Quaker closer to heart, as shown in photo, with slave woman positioned next to Woolman.*
This made Friends the first religious community in the colonies to free themselves of the burden of slave holding. By doing this, what they believed on the inside, and how they acted on the outside, became one and the same.	*Pick up gold heart, showing each side as you say "inside" and "outside."*
John Woolman treated all people with respect. He wrote about slavery so people could discuss it. He would not support an unjust system financially. He protested visibly yet peacefully. These ways of non-violent protest are still used today.	*Indicate Woolman figure tenderly.*

John Woolman led the way in showing that the Truth in our hearts and our actions in the world can be one and the same, and can change the hearts and minds of others.

Point to flame on "inside" of heart.

Pause. When you begin the wondering, look up at participants to indicate you welcome their responses.

I wonder what part of this story you like best.

I wonder what part of this story is most important to you today.

I wonder why it feels so important to dress and act like people we know.

I wonder how many people today, like John Woolman, have the integrity to refuse to buy things made by people who have not been fairly paid, even if it means being different.

I wonder how John Woolman saw so clearly that slavery is wrong before other people did.

I wonder if you have seen someone whose beliefs on the inside and actions on the outside are the same.

I wonder where you are in this story, or what part feels like it's about you.

I wonder how we can continue the work John Woolman began.

I wonder if you know someone like this.

I wonder if being a slaveholder makes a person a master. I wonder if being enslaved makes a person a slave.

Note: *It may not be appropriate to use all of these wondering questions each time, but as participants begin to respond you can get a sense of what wonderings are the right ones for the group at this time. An appropriate wondering might arise that is not listed here.*

Note to storytellers:

Language: A great deal of thought has gone into the choice of language used in this story, including consultation with Friends involved in FGC's Ministry on Racism program. Use of the words *slave* and *master* reflect the vocabulary most frequently used in children's literature on the topic of slavery in American history. The story also refers to *"people held as slaves"* to indicate that enslavement is a condition; people are not by nature slaves. For this same reason, the term owner has been avoided. We are aware that in racial justice work and academia, preferred vocabulary refers to the *enslaved person* held by an *enslaver*.

Storytellers need to consider the group who will experience the story, and use the language that is appropriate to that circle of listeners. The language of *enslaved/enslaver* is included in the wondering questions, and for adults and older children in particular, you might consider using these terms in the story as well.

Historical Background: John Woolman (1720–1772) stopped wearing dyed clothing in 1761, when he was 41 years old. His journey to Wyalusing took place in 1763. Woolman visited meetings from New England down through the Carolinas, usually accompanied by another Friend. He held a traveling letter from his home meeting (Mt Holly, NJ) in support of his mission. Friends in areas Woolman is known to have visited are encouraged to check into your Meeting's archives for reference to Woolman, or to emancipation of enslaved people.

Philadelphia Yearly Meeting, of which Woolman was a member, took these steps to end slavery among its membership: (1) 1758: any who buy or sell slaves are to be excluded from business affairs; (2) importing slaves banned; and (3) slave holding banned in 1774. New York YM allowed its members to hold Africans and their descendants in bondage up until 1777, when Friends were directed by the Yearly Meeting to manumit the people they held in slavery.

Sources

The Journal and Major Essays of John Woolman, ed. Phillips P Moulton, Friends United Press, Richmond IN, 1971.

Gummere, Amelia Mott, *The Quaker: A Study in Costume*, Benjamin Blom, New York/London, 19968. (First published 1901)

Peare, Catherine Owens, *John Woolman: Child of Light*, Vanguard Press, NY, 1954.

Slaughter, Thomas P., *The Beautiful Soul of John Woolman, Apostle of Abolition*, Hill and Wang (a division of Farrar, Strauss and Giroux), New York, 2008.

Additional Resources

The John Woolman Curriculum, ed. by Martha Smith
The 1994 John Woolman curriculum contains many ideas to supplement this story:
http://www.pym.org/publications/pym-curricula/john-woolman-curriculum/

"A Racial Justice Curriculum for Young Friends" by Lisa Graustein (Grades 7–12).
A 10-lesson curriculum helping middle and high school-aged Friends to grapple with racial justice issues beginning with their own understandings of their racial identity.
Download: www.lisag.me

As seen in photo of story materials, these 2½" height documents should be cut out and mounted on light cardboard for use in this story. The will is an actual will; and the other is a facsimile of a document Woolman helped to write.

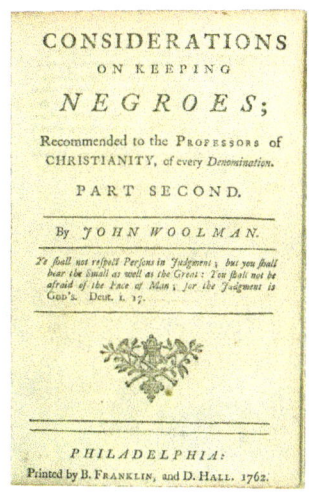

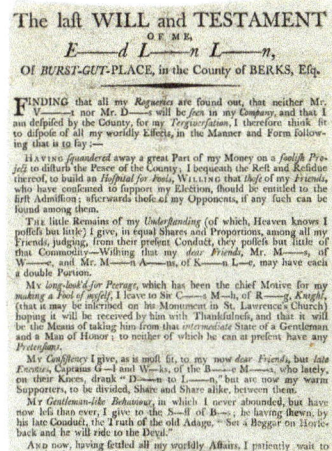

John Woolman Visits the Indians at Wyalusing

A Quaker risks a dangerous journey to visit people with lives very different from his

Photo taken from perspective of the listeners.

Materials

- Dark or forest green felt underlay approx. 24" square, rounded at the corners if you like.
- Felt shapes for mountains and blue yarn for rivers.
- 3 small mid- brown felt rectangles for settlers' homes (2" x 3") and several darker brown Indian longhouses (2" x 4") including one large longhouse (4" x 6")
- Set of Quaker figures, including Woolman figure wearing off-white color, a woman and a girl.
- 5 reddish people figures with feathers and perhaps leather to represent American Indians, including one with papoose. Optional: small tomahawk (wooden matchstick with paper head works fine)

WORDS	MOVEMENTS
[*Optional:* Watch where I go to get this story so you will always know where to find it. It's not where the sacred stories are. It's not where the parables are.]	*Get story materials and return to your place in the circle.*
This is a story of Quaker faith and witness. It is about someone who listened to the still, small voice within and discovered what God wanted him to do. His beliefs on the inside and his actions on the outside became one and the same. His actions bore witness to Truth.	
This is a story about John Woolman's visit to the American Indians at Wyalusing, Pennsylvania. He reached out in friendship to people whose lives were very different from his.	*Pause. Eyes down.*
Long ago, heavy forest covered the land. Rivers and streams were full of fish. Mountains were full of animal life. The ground was fertile for growing food. This was home to Native American Indians. They lived together in large buildings called *longhouses*.	*Set out underlay. Set out rivers and mountains.*
	Add longhouses all over, including left edge.
Then, new people began to come from far away. They built homes on this land. As more and more settlers came, they pushed the Native Americans from their homes and lands. This caused anger between the settlers and the Indians. Often fighting broke out, and people died.	*Set out settler homes at left edge, then "push" longhouses to right as shown.*
One of the settlers was a Quaker named John Woolman. He always tried to live in ways of the Spirit. He tried to see that of God in everyone, even in people others didn't like, or were afraid of. He knew it is important to be open to friendship with other people, especially those whose lives are different.	*Bring out white Woolman figure; hold him gently as you talk about him.*

Faith & Play™ | John Woolman Visits the Indians at Wyalusing

John lived in what is now New Jersey with his wife, Sarah, and their daughter, Mary. He believed deeply that all people are children of God and should be treated with respect. He had long been concerned about how most settlers treated the Indians. Often, the settlers wanted the Indians' land but did not want to pay a fair price for it.	*Place Woolman and family near a settler house.*
One day, John felt called to visit certain Indians he had met several years earlier. They lived far away, in a place called Wyalusing, in the northern part of Pennsylvania. By spending time with them, he hoped to understand more about their lives, and learn how they were like people he knew as well as how they were different. Perhaps by getting to know one another better, respect and friendship might grow between them.	*Put 3 Indians near long-house at Wyalusing; place woman with papoose just outside village.*
John prayed with Sarah and with other Friends about whether it was wise to go. They knew it would be dangerous. And they knew John would not use a weapon. In the end, Friends trusted that God truly wanted him to make this journey, at this time.	*Indicate Sarah and John.*
So John left his home and began his journey. Another Quaker and an Indian guide joined him. Many people along the way told him to turn back. Five times he questioned whether this journey should be made at this time. Five times the answer in his heart was "yes."	*Begin to move John.* *Hold up 5 fingers each time you say 5.*
This journey was not only dangerous. It was difficult, too. There were no roads back then, just a few trails through the wilderness. There were swamps to get through, mountains and rivers to cross. Wild animals lived all around. Four times rattlesnakes threatened. To make things worse, it rained and rained and rained.	*Move John on wandering path toward Wyalusing, pausing frequently.*

From time to time, they crossed paths with Indians and traders. Each time they wondered if the strangers would be friendly or not. [*Optional:* Once, when they came into a small village an Indian came toward John with a tomahawk in his hand. John did not turn away. Instead he walked toward the man with open hands and gentle greeting. The Indian lowered his tomahawk. Spirit brought them together.]	*Bring out Indian figure, and have him approach Woolman. Act out story, then put this figure away.* *Cup hands to either side of figures, like parentheses.*
After traveling for nearly ten days, John and his companions came to Wyalusing. The first person he met, just outside the village, was a woman with her baby. She and John sat on logs across from one another, and found that even though they spoke different languages they could reach out to one another in friendship. Spirit brought them together.	*Bring John close to female Indian with papoose.* *Hold hands to either side like parentheses.*
John was invited into the village. He joined the Indians every morning and evening when they gathered to talk. Often he spoke to the group, and told them of God's love for all people, and of God's desire for all people to live in peace.	*Move Woolman figure to longhouse with Indians.*
The second day, John says he "felt the current of love run strong" between them. He asked that they not translate each thing they said, and trusted the divine spirit would make the meaning clear. One Indian, named Papunehung, said he was glad to see where the words came from. Spirit brought them together.	*Repeat "parentheses" gesture.*
When the time came to leave Wyalusing, John and each Indian shook hands in friendship. He also shook hands with some who had not been part of the meetings, to show he felt friendship for them, too.	*Bring figures together in pairs, as if shaking hands.*
When John Woolman turned toward home, many Indians accompanied him for part of the journey. They traveled together, mostly by canoe, along the rivers.	*Move figures back toward your left, using rivers when possible. Take your time.*

Faith & Play™ | John Woolman Visits the Indians at Wyalusing

When they came near farms, the Quakers were careful to walk ahead. They did not want settlers to be frightened of these friendly Indians or want to harm them.

At last, the Indians returned to their home at Wyalusing and John to his in West Jersey.

Return figures to their homes.

In his journal, John Woolman expressed deep gratitude for the respect and affection between the Indians and himself. He felt he had done what God asked of him by reaching out to the Indians in friendship.

Use parentheses gesture.

Spirit brought them together.

Pause. When you begin the wondering, look up at participants to indicate you welcome their responses.

I wonder which part of this story you like best.

I wonder what is most important for you today.

I wonder where you are in this story, or what part is about you.

I wonder if there is any part we could leave out, and still have all the story we need.

I wonder why it is so important to be friendly with people who are different from us.

I wonder if you ever feel a connection with people different from you.

I wonder why it can seem so difficult to reach out to people different from us.

I wonder what would happen if we reached out to people different from us more often.

I wonder if you have ever heard God ask you to do something difficult or dangerous.

I wonder which testimonies John's actions show.

I wonder if you know someone like this.

Note to storytellers:

John Woolman (1720–72) was born and lived near Mount Holly, New Jersey. He devoted much of his life to treating all people as equal, regardless of their race or condition.

We know about this story from reading John Woolman's journal, which was written more than 200 years ago and is still being read today.

This story takes place in 1763, during the French and Indian Wars (1756–63). His destination, Wyalusing ("Y"-uh-LOO- sing), is located in north central Pennsylvania, on the banks of the Susquehanna River. This area and nearby were major centers of conflict at that time.

The man who went with Woolman was Benjamin Parvin. The indigenous people in this story are Delaware Indians. With the exception of Papunehung (pa-POO-na-hung), their names are not known.

Some children may ask why the Woolman figure is dressed in white rather than Quaker grey. The short answer is that John Woolman chose to wear only cloth which had not been dyed, because producing dyes involved the labor of enslaved people, and he did not wish to support slavery in any way. Another Faith & Play™ story, "John Woolman, Gentle Abolitionist," tells more about this part of Woolman's life.

Sources

The Journal and Major Essays of John Woolman, ed. Phillips P Moulton, Friends United Press, Richmond IN, 1971.

Peare, Catherine Owens, *John Woolman: Child of Light*, Vanguard Press, NY, 1954.

Slaughter, Thomas P., *The Beautiful Soul of John Woolman, Apostle of Abolition*, Hill and Wang (a division of Farrar, Strauss and Giroux), New York, 2008.

Other Resources

See also Philadelphia Yearly Meeting's 1994 John Woolman curriculum for many ideas to supplement this story. May be borrowed from PYM library.

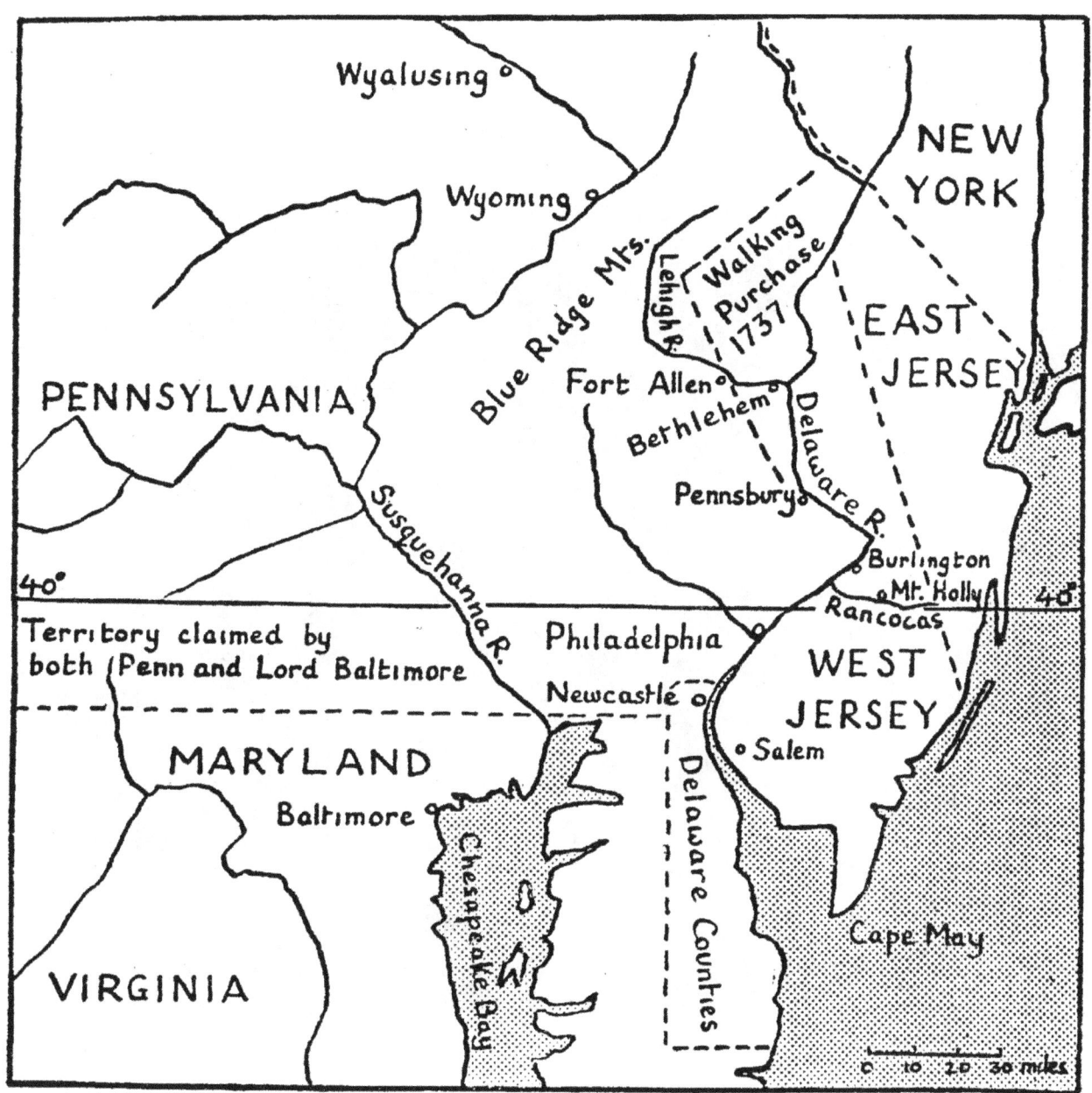

PENNSYLVANIA AND NEW JERSEY IN THE TIME OF PENN AND WOOLMAN.

Map, originally published as part of Philadelphia Yearly Meeting's *The Woolman Curriculum*, used with permission.

Elizabeth Fry and the Women of Newgate Prison

How she saw people opened the door to prison reform

Photo taken from perspective of the listeners.

Materials

- Meadow green felt underlay approximately 24" x 20"; black rectangle approximately 8" x 10" for prison; brown or tan felt for Fry house, 5" x 9" with sloped roof as in photo.
- People figures: Elizabeth Fry with lace shawl; 8–10 female "prisoners" including mother with infant and several children.
- Small bits of flannel to suggest children's nightshirts; several "blankets" and a quilt; a spool of thread; small book and blackboard; small bucket or tub.

WORDS	MOVEMENTS
[*Optional*: Watch where I go to get this story so you will always know where to find it. It's not where the sacred stories are. It's not where the parables are.]	*Get story materials from the Quaker story area and return to your place in the circle. Put story materials beside you.*
This is a story of Quaker faith and witness. It is about someone who listened to the still, small voice within and discovered what God wanted her to do. Her beliefs on the inside and her actions on the outside became one and the same. Her actions bore witness to Truth.	*Hold one hand palm up for "inside," other palm up for "outside." Bring palms together in prayer position for "same."*
This story is about Elizabeth Fry, a woman who reached out with kindness to women in prison, and began a major change in how we treat people in jail.	*Smooth out green felt underlay.*
This story takes place in England long after the time of George Fox and Margaret Fell and Mary Fisher.	*Take out and show Elizabeth figure.*
Elizabeth Fry was a Quaker lady. She came from a wealthy, educated family with a large and comfortable home and active lives. As an adult, she lived in London with her husband, a banker, and their children.	*Set out Fry house and put Elizabeth in it.*
Not far from her home was a large, old prison called Newgate. It was the same prison where George Fox, William Penn and other Friends had been imprisoned for living their faith.	*Set out felt for Newgate.* *Long pause as you look at Newgate.*
Prison is a harsh place. No one goes there unless they have to. Prisoners are locked away from home and family and friends. There are no comforts, and no comfort, in prison.	*Touch prison.*
One day, a Friend who had visited Newgate described the conditions to Elizabeth. People were penned up in large rooms, as if they were animals.	
	Pause.
The prison was crowded. Cold. Dirty. And noisy. Plus there were children—even infants—in prison with their mothers.	

Elizabeth was troubled. She was especially distressed that babies and children were there. So she decided to visit Newgate herself to see what could be done.

Move Elizabeth to prison.

At first, the jailer did not want to let her in. "This is no place for a lady," he said. "The women here are dangerous. They could tear you apart."

Gesture "stop" with your hand.

But Elizabeth insisted, and at last he let them in.

Advance Elizabeth into the prison.

Inside, Elizabeth saw for herself that it was as she feared. It was crowded. It was cold and dirty. It was noisy.

Begin placing prisoners in jail, helter skelter, some lying down. Pause here for a few moments to reflect on what Elizabeth saw there.

But maybe that isn't all she saw. Perhaps she saw fellow human beings who had experienced difficulty, and were still capable of change for the good. Women who were mothers, sisters, daughters, wives, each with that of God within.

Touch several figures gently near heart.

Then she noticed a sick child in its mother's arms. Her heart melted. She reached out and gently touched the child's head. "What dost thou need?" she asked softly.

Gently touch child with your finger.

Her concern was so real that the women trusted her. She spoke to many women that day, hearing their stories and showing her care for them. She read the Bible aloud, and spoke of God's love for all people. When she left, she promised to return and do more to help them.

Move Elizabeth back to "home" area.

And so the journey began. Elizabeth could not do everything herself. So she spoke to other Quaker women. Together they did many things to help the prisoners. They brought blankets to keep the prisoners warm, and clothing.

Place a stack of blankets in the jail area.

They arranged for the women to have water to wash with.

Set out bucket or tub.

Elizabeth also encouraged the women to work together, in teams, to help one another. The prison began to feel different: safer and more orderly.

Gather the prisoners in orderly pairs and small groups.

In time, the Quaker women taught the women to sew clothing for themselves and their children.	*Place a small spool of thread near the women.*
The women learned to make quilts to sell when they got out of prison, to make money.	*Set out a small patchwork "quilt."*
The children and the grown-ups learned to read and do basic arithmetic.	*Place small book & slate in the area.*
The prisoners began to see themselves differently. They had hope that they could make their way in the world beyond prison walls. Maybe they could even see That of God in themselves and each other.	*Touch several figures in heart area.* *Pause.*
Elizabeth Fry reached out a caring hand to women who had known little kindness and respect in their lives. She saw That of God in them, and that made all the difference in the world.	*Gesture from Elizabeth to prisoners.*
Her work led to prison reform in England and Europe and America and all over the world. Elizabeth Fry's story of Quaker faith and witness continues today as Friends still visit prisons to speak to that of God in every person.	
	Pause. When you begin the wondering, look up at participants to indicate you welcome their responses.
I wonder what part of this story you like best.	
I wonder what part is most important to you today.	
I wonder where you are in this story, or what part of the story is about you.	
I wonder how the women in prison felt when Elizabeth Fry first came to Newgate.	
I wonder what words you would use to describe Elizabeth Fry.	
I wonder if there are people in your Meeting who visit prison.	
I wonder if you know someone like this.	

Note to storytellers:

Prior to the ministry of Elizabeth Gurney Fry (1780–1845), people who had been jailed were regarded as fallen from grace and beyond redemption. In England, prisoners were routinely exiled and shipped off to Australia, far from friends, family and familiar surroundings. As a result of her work, people who were jailed began to be viewed as capable of becoming useful members of society once again. It would be difficult to exaggerate the importance of her work.

Fry is one of only two women other than Queen Elizabeth II to appear on British currency (five-pound note). The friend who brought her news of Newgate was Stephen Grellet, a French/American Quaker. Her friend Anna Buxton was at this meeting and accompanied Elizabeth on her first visit to the prison. Her brother was Joseph John Gurney.

Sources

Swiss, Deborah, "The Angel of the Prisons: Elizabeth Gurney Fry"; *Friends Journal,* March 2012, Philadelphia, PA.

Elizabeth Fry: A Quaker Life, ed. by Gil Skidmore, Rowman & Littlefield, 2005.

Elizabeth Fry: Britain's Second Lady on the Five Pound Note, by Dennis Bardens, Chanadon Publications, Ltd., London, 2004.

Elizabeth Fry, Quaker Heroine, by Janet Whitney, Little, Brown & Co, Boston, 1936.

"The Boot Under the Bed"(pp. 9–11) and "Elizabeth Fry" (pp. 117–125) in *Lighting Candles in the Dark: Stories of Courage and Love in Action,* Friends General Conference, 1992, 2001.

Other Stories for Friends

An Easter Story for Friends

A story about the power of God's love

Photo taken from perspective of the listeners.

Materials

- ❍ White circle underlay (approximately 24" in diameter) made of felt or heavy cotton.
- ❍ 12" x 18" cross shape made of wood, stiff felt or foam (black on one side and purple on the other) and cut into 6 pieces that fit together like a puzzle (see photo):
  - ❐ the top piece has a flame on the purple side and the black side is blank;
  - ❐ the center piece has Jesus on the purple side and a tomb on the black side;
  - ❐ the piece to the right of Jesus (viewer's perspective) has a baby chick on purple and an egg on the black side;
  - ❐ the piece to the left of Jesus (viewer's perspective) has a butterfly on purple and a cocoon on the black side;
  - ❐ the piece below Jesus has a tree in leaf on purple and bare branches of a tree on the black side;
  - ❐ the piece below the tree has fresh, spring-green grass on the purple side and dried brown grass on black.

| WORDS | MOVEMENTS |

This is a story about the mystery of Easter.

Lay out underlay.

A mystery can be hard to understand. Sometimes we just need to listen, and to watch and to breathe in the mystery before it begins to open to us. Mystery means there are things that happen that we don't understand, and can't explain.

What do we have here to help us get ready for the mystery of Easter? What could this be? And this? What could these all be? Maybe it is a puzzle. A puzzle is a kind of mystery.

*Turn to basket. Take out pieces of cross, black side up. Place randomly around underlay, **except tomb/Jesus piece still in basket**. (Do not form cross shape, yet.)*

Sometimes it's difficult to come close to a mystery. We need to wonder about many things.

"Play" with the pieces, black-side up. Move them around to different places.

During this time of year, when spring is bringing new life to the world again, there are many mysteries to wonder about.

We wonder how the earth knows when to leave winter and turn into spring. We wonder how light can come from darkness. What **power** could be great enough to tell the earth when to leave the darkness of winter and change into spring?

Turn over flame piece.
Indicate flame when you say "power."

[As you read the questions that come next, turn over each corresponding piece on the underlay.]

How does a baby bird know it's time to break **free** from the egg? How does a tree that had dark, empty branches in the winter, start to **grow** leaves? How does the grass **come back to life** and turn green again? How do caterpillars, **alone** in their cocoons, turn into butterflies?

The world is made new again.

Indicate pieces with your hand, like a blessing (bird, butterfly, tree).

I wonder if we can take these pieces and make them into a shape that means Easter.

Move pieces (now purple-side up) into the shape of a cross, with the center piece still missing.

Ah, there is one more piece to help us, the one at the center of Easter.	*Take out piece with purple/Jesus side up.*
The baby who was born at Christmas grew to be a man named Jesus, who said wonderful things and did amazing things. People began to follow him and wanted to know more. He taught about love and forgiveness. He showed God's love for all people in the way he lived.	*Hold up and indicate Jesus figure.* *Place Jesus piece in center of cross.*
There are many symbols that crowd around Easter, but at the center of Easter is the symbol of a cross.	*Trace puzzle cross with your finger.*
When Jesus died on the cross the people were sad. His body was taken and placed in a tomb, and a heavy stone was rolled over the doorway.	*Pick up Jesus piece and turn over to tomb side. Trace stone with finger.*
Then a mysterious thing happened. People found that Jesus was still with them, in a wondrous new way. When we come close to the mystery of Easter there is the living Jesus, a Light for the world.	*Turn back over to the purple side; return piece to center of cross.*
He shows us the power of God's love to transform...	*At "power" touch flame.*
...death to life ...darkness to light ...sadness to joy ...hurt to forgiveness ...hatred to love ...winter into spring.	*Pause.*
God's love is for everyone. Jesus showed us the power of his love, and his words and work are still with us today. Spring returns each year and brings back light and life. God is always with us.	*Gesture toward flame.* *Touch Jesus at center of story. Indicate chick, tree, grass, butterfly. Hold out hands to encircle whole story.* *Pause. When you begin the wondering, look up at participants to indicate you welcome their responses.*

Faith & Play™ | An Easter Story for Friends

I wonder what part of the story you like best.

I wonder what part is the most important for you, today.

I wonder where you are in the story or what part feels like it is about you.

I wonder how you feel when you see new life in springtime.

I wonder how the baby bird feels when it breaks free of the egg for the first time.

I wonder how the tree feels when at last it sprouts new leaves.

I wonder how the grass feels when it turns green again.

I wonder how the caterpillar feels, after all that time in a cocoon, when it turns into a butterfly.

I wonder where you have known the Light.

I wonder how you have experienced God's love.

I wonder how it feels to be forgiven, and start all over again.

I wonder what you wonder about this story.

Sources

This story is adapted for Friends from the Godly Play® story "The Mystery of Easter" (*The Complete Guide to Godly Play*, Volume 4: *20 Presentations for Spring*, by Jerome W. Berryman © 2003) and work by the Faith & Play™ Group and its corresponding members.

Materials: Another Look

Another look at materials made using two sheets of foam (black and purple) glued together; felt shapes and figures were cut out and adhered to the pieces.

Faith & Play™ | An Easter Story for Friends

Appendices

Resources for the Faith & Play™ Teacher

Print Materials

Teaching Godly Play: How to Mentor the Spiritual Development of Children, Jerome Berryman (Morehouse, revised and expanded 2009). This book illustrates how to establish a Montessori approach to religious education that encourages children to seek and find their own answers to their faith questions. It is a primary source for understanding the practice of Godly Play®.

Godly Play: An Imaginative Approach to Religious Education, Jerome Berryman (Augsburg Fortress Publishers, 1995) This publication presents the theory and theology underpinning Godly Play®.

The Complete Guide to Godly Play (series), Jerome Berryman (Morehouse Education Resources)

Volume 1: How to Lead Godly Play Lessons Provides essential information about the Godly Play® approach, including how to create a special space for children, planning and presenting Godly Play® stories and helping children's spiritual development. (2002)

Volume 2: Presentations for Fall Includes an opening lesson and Old Testament stories covering Creation through the Prophets. (2002, revised 2017)

Volume 3: Presentations for Winter Includes stories based on stories of Jesus's birth and the parables. (2002, revised 2017)

Volume 4: Presentations for Spring Includes more stories from the life of Jesus, including his death and resurrection. (2003, revised 2017)

Volume 5: Practical Helps from Godly Play Trainers Experienced teachers and trainers share insights, stories and ideas for using Godly Play® to its fullest potential. (2003)

Volume 6: Additional Enrichment Lessons to Supplement Fall Includes 15 presentations about the people of God, including stories about Abraham, Sarah, Moses and Ruth. (2006)

Volume 7: Enrichment Presentations Includes 16 story presentations on the lives of saints of the church. This volume will be of negligible use to Friends, but the First Day School teacher might want to use one or two of the stories, such as of St. Valentine. The volume provides a format for having children write the stories of their own lives. (2008)

Volume 8: New Core and Enrichment Sessions This final volume in the series includes supplementary material summarizing the literature about Godly Play® as well as an overview of the entire curriculum. (August 2012)

Young Children and Worship, Sonja M. Stewart and Jerome Berryman (Westminster, 1989) This book provides story texts to help 3–8 year old children discover what meaning certain Bible stories have for them. (The story materials are similar to those used in some Godly Play® stories.)

Following Jesus, Sonja M. Stewart (Geneva Press, 2000). A follow-up to *Young Children and Worship*, this volume presents stories of the life of Jesus as well as his parables. Friends may find helpful some of the patterns for story materials that are provided at the back of the book.

Jugar llenos de fe: Relatos de los cuáqueros para los Amigos entrenados en el método de Jugar Junto a Dios® is the Spanish translation of Faith & Play™ stories published by New England Yearly Meeting and available as a free download on their website: **neym.org/qye/jugar-llenos-fe**

Web Resources

www.facebook.com/FaithandPlay Facebook page for the Faith & Play™ community of practice across the globe. Supported by the Faith & Play™ Group, news and announcements about trainings are posted here, as well as Friends sharing questions and experiences with Faith & Play™ and Godly Play®.

www.fgcquaker.org/faith-and-play Pages on the Friends General Conference website with information and resources about Faith & Play™ and Godly Play® for Friends.

www.godlyplayfoundation.org This is the official site for Godly Play® information in the United States and home of the Center for the Theology of Childhood. 503-915-5755

Teacher Training

Godly Play® and Faith & Play™ are best shared and implemented in programs by Friends who have attended training. Many Friends describe their experience of attending a *Playing in the Light: Godly Play® and Faith & Play™ Training** as spiritual retreat as well as a workshop for learning new skills. Trainings are an opportunity to gather with a community of practitioners, deepen your practice, and gain clarity about the "hows and whys" of the Godly Play® method.

Everything the storyteller says and does in the Godly Play® and Faith & Play™ classroom are for a reason. Storytellers must have a comfortable understanding of the philosophy and methodology used in this approach. Even teachers of young children, experienced storytellers, and those who have already begun exploring using Godly Play® and Faith & Play™ stories benefit from training for these stories to be experienced as they were intended.

Training is available for both Friends in local meetings and teachers in Friends schools who wish to use Godly Play® and Faith & Play™ in their religious education or Quaker studies programs. To learn more about workshops and how you might benefit, please contact faithandplaystories@gmail.com.

>*Teachers can also get foundational training in Godly Play® (but not Faith & Play™) through the Godly Play® Foundation.

> "I had taught on the kindergarten, elementary and college level, and had experience teaching First Day School and leading workshops. I was an experienced teacher. After participating in two or three Godly Play® lessons at an ecumenical teachers' event, I was deeply moved and inspired by the experience. Feeling I had a good grasp of the concept and an adequate understanding of the basic technique I began experimenting with Godly Play®, even telling the stories in Quaker workshops. It was not until several years later, when I received training and was certified as a Godly Play® teacher, that I realized I had not, in fact, adequately understood the hows and whys and whens of Godly Play® during those years of experimentation. Only after that weekend training was I able to write the drafts that, after diligent testing and editing with other trained storytellers, became some of the first Faith & Play™ stories in publication."
>
> — *Michael Gibson*

A Story Session Outline for Friends

Adapted for Friends from the work of Jerome Berryman

by Melinda Wenner Bradley, Godly Play® Trainer

The story session in many ways models the experience of attending worship among Friends. We cross a threshold into sacred space to worship together in community. We gather to experience God in the messages and music in programmed worship, or sit together in the silence of waiting worship to hear how God moves us to speak. We are a community of listeners and storytellers, sharing our questions and our Truth. The outline below is a guide to the "parts of the lesson," and Friends may adapt this outline as fits the needs of their work with Faith & Play™ or Godly Play® stories. It is not meant as a prescription but an explanatory guide, and we hope you will be most faithful to how Spirit moves among you and the children.

Entrance: Gathering and Getting Ready

○ *Greeting at the threshold (by the door-keeper)*

Whether it is a doorway into a room, or stepping over a created "threshold" like a stick laid on the ground, there should be a sense of crossing into sacred space. Stories can be told anywhere — a room, outside, in a worship space or home. We can create a sense that the place where the story will be told is special, whether we visit there once or many times, by asking children to pause and be welcomed. Before they even enter the space we ask if they are **ready**; ready to listen, to wonder, and to do their work. The person who greets the children (the "door person") should be seated at their eye level, be friendly and greet them by name, if possible. They are being welcomed into a special time together in a

> The Faith & Play™ stories were written for a religious education context where God is the language used, and for storytellers using Godly Play®. Storytellers may need to be flexible and adapt that language to make space for using the stories in their community. However, in some cases, keeping God language in the parts of the story that refer to historic context and experience are important; for example in "George Fox's Big Discovery," references to Fox's experience of spiritual opening.
>
> This introduction before the story is something developed with teachers at Friends schools and with Friends in meetings where God is not the preferred language for stories. You are welcome to adapt it further for your own community:
>
> *"Here at [name of school/meeting] we believe that there is a spark of the Divine, or an inner light, in everyone. Some people call this God, and other people use other names like Allah or HaShem. Some people call this the Divine, or Great Spirit or simply love. There is a light in each of us."*

special place that is for them. It is the first step into being in spiritual community together in the circle.

- *Entering the circle of children*

    Children are invited to sit in the circle with the storyteller-teacher. The storyteller-teacher greets each child, too. Sometimes you invite a child to a particular spot, near you or across from you.

- *Engaging with the community (introductions and sharing)*

    Welcome everyone. Go around the circle and be sure everyone is introduced by name, or ask a simple question. (How was your week? What do you like about spring?) You are inviting them to be a community in the circle, to know one another as Friends.

The Story: Hearing, Listening, Responding

- *Bringing the story into the circle (from the shelves)*

    "Watch where I go . . ." Whether you are in a classroom with stories or in a space with one story, there is language at the beginning of the words for you to use.

- *Listening*

    Invite the children to settle their bodies and voices, and get ready to listen to the story. You may need to remind them that you will be looking at the story materials, and they can, too. If they have questions or comments during the story, they can hold them in their hearts until you wonder about the story together.

- *Presenting the story*

    Out of the gathered silence, present the story. Take your time, there is no need to hurry as the children are listening and entering the story themselves. When working with the story materials, be tender and gentle. Your respect for the materials and for the story is important modeling for the children.

- *Wondering*

    Leave the story materials out as you wonder together. This way, you can use pieces from the story to think about it, play with the ideas and questions children express in the wondering time.

    Invite the children to explore the story with the wondering questions. Wondering is about openness and dialogue, there are no right or wrong answers. Keep in mind that giving your own interpretations or thoughts closes the wondering and any possible meaning that children might discover for themselves. Making meaning is a process and a journey. Any reflection on their wondering should model openness and not judgment; you don't have to have all the answers, either! "I hadn't thought of that." "I wonder about that, too." "Hmm." Always, wondering happens on the inside first; some children are not ready to wonder out loud with the circle. Make space for silence, and do not rush or call on children to answer. We are modeling for them so many things about our faith as Friends: silence, waiting, listening, and remaining open to Truth.

- *Returning the story*

    Take your time to put the story pieces back into the basket or box that contains it. If you have shelves for stories in a room, return the story to its place there. If you do not have stories on shelves, or are in a space with just that story, set it aside. In either case, children may want to work with it during the response time.

- *Working individually*

    After the story, children have a choice of what they would like to work with to continue wondering about the story they heard. The storyteller-teacher provides structure and boundaries, as they do during the story. Make this time as orderly as possible, asking each child in the circle, "I wonder what your work will be?" Dismiss the children one at a time to select their work and bring it back to their place in the circle. The door-keeper assists the child, if needed, to find, gather, and use materials appropriately.

    You could have some art supplies for them to use, they could work with the story you told or others that are available in the space you're using. Their work time might also include reading the Bible or quietly resting. This is a time for them to discern what they would like to do, not a time for you to direct them. Make their choices clear, and let them decide. Some children may need you to show them how to use a material, or want you to retell a story for them. Others may tell stories to one another, or work with two stories together.

    Also note that children are not asked to share their work or any product of it. The focus is on **process**, and we do not evaluate their work. Sometimes, children want to show you what they are doing or have made; in your response, be affirming and non-judgmental, as you are in the wondering. "Yes, it's a lot of blue." "You mixed many colors." "You've rearranged parts of the story materials to make something new."

    > **A comment on art supplies:** Like the story materials you create, the art materials for the response time should be selected and displayed with care. Focus on a simple selection that is the finest quality you can provide. It does not need to be expensive or fancy; natural materials are beautiful and invitational. Having a supply of well-kept materials lovingly displayed communicates to the participants that they are valued and appreciated, and that the work they will be doing is important. The array of supplies can also stimulate their imagination. Some suggestions: pencils, colored pencils, paints, clay, feathers, yarn, paper, glue, and scissors. Keep scraps as the supplies are used; they will be put to good use.

- *Putting away work and materials*

    The children should share in the clean up and care for the space you have used. They put stories back in their places and return other materials where they found them, and return to the circle.

The Feast: Preparing and Sharing (optional)

This section of the lesson is optional; you may not always have time for it in First Day School or a story presentation. The idea of the "feast" is communal experience; it is the community of the circle of children doing work together by sharing a simple snack or a song. It is not, however, meant to be a Eucharist for children. Follow the practices of your Friends church or meeting. Another kind of communal work is to sing a song together — lifting up voices in a feast of sound and words.

- *Preparing to share*

    If sharing food, the children serve the napkins, cups, and food to the group. The doorkeeper should help the children to serve one another by handing out items from a tray or container that they can carry themselves. They can take turns and help one another.

- *Grace (communal thanks)*

    The circle might share grace out loud or have a moment of silence. You might remind the children that prayers can be said in many ways, with our voice or in our hearts.

- *Sharing a simple snack (or a song)*

    The storyteller reminds the children that we wait until everyone is served and ready. "What makes a feast is not what we have, or how much we have, but that we share it together." This is a time to enjoy being together, sharing and listening in quiet conversation.

- *Cleaning up*

    Remember, the children should be the ones to clean up; show them how, and allow them to do it themselves.

Closing: Rise of Meeting and Going Forth

At the end of your time together, you might have a brief period of worship or silent prayer, closing with shaking of hands in the manner of Friends. The children might be invited to stand and hold hands, or they might sit and then exchange hand shakes at the end, as is done at the rise of worship.

- *Leaving the circle*

    Children are thanked for their presence and participation, and dismissed from the circle in the same way they joined it, with the help of the storyteller-teacher. They return to the door-keeper to be sent out from the space, to return to parents or join the adults in worship.

- *Afterward*

    The storyteller and door-keeper might have a discussion of how the lesson went and observations of the children and their work. They may want to make some written notes about the session. What went well? What would you like to do differently next time?

Getting Started with a Circle
Introducing the Godly Play® or Faith & Play™ Story Session

by Melinda Wenner Bradley, Godly Play® Trainer

After participating in a training, you go home and prepare to introduce stories into your First Day or Friends school program. It's helpful to consider how to introduce the method/structure before you share a Godly Play® or Faith & Play™ story with your circle of children. Children are best supported when they understand expectations, and it is often better to show and experience the process in steps taken together, rather than only describe it to them with words.

Start with introducing the parts which "frame" a story session. Begin with guidance about with how the children enter the space: Have someone be a door person for you, and invite children to cross a "threshold" into the space where they will hear stories. It doesn't need to be a doorway, but should be an intentional place to stop and ask, "Are you ready?" and introduce the idea of getting ready. You could even do this yourself — make it an adventure, start outside the room — "We're going to be hearing stories in a new way, and we need to get ready, can you do this with me?"

Enter the space with intention, talking about how to be ready, and then build the circle. Take some time to share around the circle (names if needed, favorite colors, things they like about the season, etc.) to build community and let children practice hearing their voices in the circle. If you're not yet ready to share a Godly Play®/Faith & Play™ story, you could read a children's picture book to them and wonder about that story as a way to introduce the wondering questions. Wondering is so different from what children are often asked to do in school classrooms (have correct answers). Re-read training handouts about wondering ("Wondering with Children: Making Space for Growing in the Light"); it's often a new skill for us, leading this part of the story session. It's been thoughtful, intentional work for me to deepen my skill at leading wondering, and I'm still learning. But the basic wondering questions used in Godly Play® Sacred Stories and most Faith & Play™ stories are good with any story, including children's books. You could start there, to introduce and practice together. (*I wonder what part of the story you liked best; I wonder what part felt most important to you; I wonder where you are in the story or what part felt like it was about you; I wonder what we could take out and still have all we need in this story.*)

When I shared Faith & Play™ stories at a local Friends school once a month, we began the year with a familiar classroom teacher bringing the group to the threshold of the meetinghouse space, and then asking each child if they were ready before they entered and joined the circle (I was waiting there for them, seated on the floor). After sharing names around the circle, my introduction to this new experience needed to be quick — I told them that just like when a book is read to them, we would use our ears and eyes for these stories, but there weren't book pages to look at, instead there would be story pieces from my basket that I would put on the floor in front of me (I showed them the basket and their eyes got big!). I invited them to use their ears to listen and their eyes to look at the story on the floor, because I would look there, too. And while we needed our ears and eyes, we would not use our voices until *after* the story — and then, we would wonder about the story together. If anyone forgot, and spoke up during the story, that was OK — they would remember better next time and we would help each other. But if they had a question or comment, I asked them to please "hold it in their heart" until the story was over, and when I look up at you, we'll share. Children were able to participate fully and comfortably from that start, because the expectations were clear and there was spaciousness as well.

    Keep in mind that you don't need to do it all at once, or introduce all the language used with this method the first or second time you share a story. We talk about being ready, and refer to their "work" when they think they're making art or playing with stories — this is language you may need to explain, and hopefully you will experience joy as you see how it truly affirms them!

Thoughts on Story Materials for Faith & Play™ and Godly Play®

1. Getting Started with Materials

Preparing materials is another way that we enter a story deeply. The photographs of story materials provided in our Faith & Play™ publication can give you ideas for creating your own materials for these stories. Building a classroom of materials is a joyful process, but might also feel daunting. You do not need a complete classroom to begin telling stories. Begin with one story; make the next one you need, and the next. The space where Godly Play® and Faith & Play™ are being used has the stories that children have heard accessible for them to choose as their work after the story and wondering. You don't need to make available stories children have not heard yet — you can build as you go. As you experience stories together, grow the classroom of materials.

2. Resources

QuakerBooks of Friends General Conference
www.quakerbooks.org or 800-966-4556

QuakerBooks of FGC stocks Faith & Play™ resources, as well as Godly Play® written resources and related materials. QuakerBooks carries Faith & Play™ story kits that require minimal finishing.

Godly Play Resources
www.godlyplayresources.com or 800-445-4390

From this website you can purchase materials for any of the Godly Play® stories in *The Complete Guide to Godly Play Volumes 1–8*. You will also find prints/kits to support creating your own materials, and the photographs on the site are another guide.

Godly Play Finland
www.godlyplay.fi/english.html

You can purchase beautiful handcrafted story materials from this website or get ideas for making your own.

The Community
www.facebook.com/FaithandPlay

The Faith & Play™ page on Facebook is a place where questions, ideas, and suggestions for finding and making story materials are shared by our community of practice.

    If you are not "crafty," look to others within your meeting or school. There may well be someone who is a woodworker, painter, sculptor, or craftsperson who would be delighted to serve the community by creating story materials. This might be older youth who have experienced the stories and can experience them in a different way by helping to make materials and contribute to the community. Even if you are proficient at crafting your own materials, you might want to invite others to contribute to the life of the meeting in this way. It could be a blessing to someone. A few visits to yard sales can yield a nice collection of baskets in which you can store the materials for each story. Within your meeting community, quarter, or yearly meeting, or Friends school, there may be visual artists who would be happy to make suggestions for art materials and help you obtain them at reasonable prices.

3. Quality and Approach

Story materials should be of the nicest quality you can buy or create, and simple in their color and shape. Wood is preferable to plastic, and simplicity of form leads to children using their imagination more fully. When working with story materials, be tender and gentle. Your respect for the materials and for the stories is important modeling for the children.

Art Response Supplies:

Art materials provided for story response should be of the finest quality your meeting or school can afford. Include as wide a range of media as is feasible for each setting, but without overwhelming the children. Possibilities include coloring pencils, markers, paints, clay, feathers, yarn, and a variety of solid and patterned papers. You may want to vary the assortment of media from time to time.

Having simple trays available for young children to transport their supplies is often beneficial, and these can sometimes be obtained secondhand from restaurant suppliers or cafeterias. Trays provide a hard surface when participants will be working on carpeted floors. They also facilitate clean-up when working with paints.

4. People Figures in Faith & Play™ Stories

Many Faith & Play™ stories employ standing 3-dimensional figures to represent people. While other materials could be chosen, we most frequently use wood, which is durable, attractive and easy to work with. We find that using unfinished, pre-made wooden figures about 4″ tall work very well. These are available at craft stores in an assortment of sizes and shapes, and online from resources like www.craftparts.com. Smaller wooden figures are available to represent children and even babies.

Skin tones can be achieved in a variety of ways. Wax shoe polish is fast and results in pleasing tones, as do wood stain pens. A note on paste wax: browns, black and tans all work well, as does mahogany to get a reddish effect. We find it best to avoid cordovan (too purple) and oxblood (too pink). No hair or facial features are needed. For some stories (*Listening for God, Prayer & Friends Meeting for Worship, Love's Way*, etc.) a red dot can be painted on the figure's chest to represent the Light within. Note that some Friends choose not to use the image of the red dot on figures.

Clothing can be made using fabric (usually felt because it has body and does not fray at the edges) or by painting the figures. For Quaker figures, grey paint in a variety of shades of grey is quick and easy. (Be sure to look for non-toxic paint.) The pattern for a woman's dress follows. This pattern can also be used for the sultan's attendants in the Mary Fisher story. Quaker men's hats and women's bonnets can be made from grey felt (patterns follow). For the American Indians in the Woolman Visits Wyalusing story, painting the figures tan to represent buckskin will differentiate their clothing. A feather and small strip of suede or rawhide can be glued on heads.

Use your imagination, don't be afraid to experiment and have fun! Children seem to love the little people, and have no trouble knowing what they represent.

5. Underlays

The piece of fabric used under the story materials sets the stage for the story and defines the place for listeners to focus their visual attention. The size should be comfortable for the storyteller and large enough to be visible to the circle of listeners. The colors of the underlays have been selected with care to represent unified themes or geographic setting. For example, the color of the three testimonies stories should be the same, representing the connected content. Felt is suggested for underlays, if available.

Instructions and Templates for Materials

Man's Quaker Hat

1. Cut two pieces of felt as shown, one for the brim, one for the crown. Heavy felt it easier to work with than standard weight felt. Manila file folder is great for making templates. Brim is a circle with radius of 3 cm, slits in middle to accommodate head. Crown is rectangle with long edge being 9.5 cm (to accommodate head with 9cm circumference, plus overlap) and 2cm height.
2. Cut slits in the center of the brim large enough to accommodate the head of the figure.
3. Sew the ends of the crown together with a few hand stitches, ending with a double stitch that won't slip. Then run a basting stitch around the top (shorter) edge and pull tight, bringing the edges together to form the crown. Tie off tightly.
4. If you are using the **heavy-weight felt**, run a little fabric glue around the inside of the crown and the top of the center brim. Place the crown on top of the brim; turn upside-down and push the "pie slices" in the center of the brim pieces up into the crown and squeeze into place. You're done!
5. Alternately, if you're using **regular-weight felt**, you will need to use a fabric-stiffening agent, readily available at a sewing store. Prepare the 2 pieces per #1–3 above. Then soak the pieces in the stiffening agent, which is white but dries clear. (Gloves are recommended — it's a little messy.) You will need to use a people figure covered in plastic wrap as a form. Squeeze all the liquid you can out of each piece. Arrange the brim on the head; shape the crown. Let each dry enough that the glue will work. Then glue the two pieces together and allow the hat to dry. Done!

Woman's Quaker Bonnet

There are 2 basic patterns for women's bonnets. Both are simple; the choice is up to you which to use. Or perhaps a few of each would serve well. The grey garb was not a uniform! In the same way, some choose to paint the doll bodies grey, and some use fabric. Either is fine. Also good to vary the shade of grey.

1. The first bonnet is made from a large half-circle of grey felt. Run stitches around the round edge then pull the thread to gather fabric so that it fits around the back of the doll's head. Take a few stitches to hold in place. Tack the front with a few stitches to hold the bonnet on head, or attach with ribbon if desired.
2. The second produces a larger bonnet that covers the neck and shoulders in back. Cut per pattern below. Pinch along dotted lines and either sew or glue in place. Tack the front with a few stitches to hold the bonnet on head, or attach with ribbon if desired.

Man's Quaker Hat

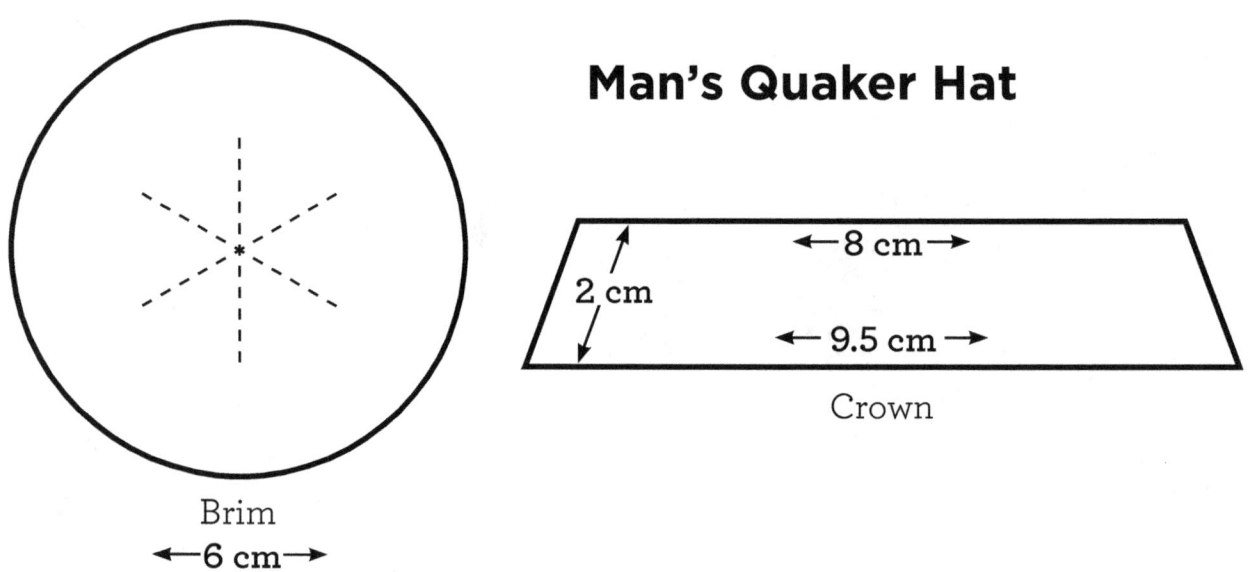

Women's Quaker Bonnet

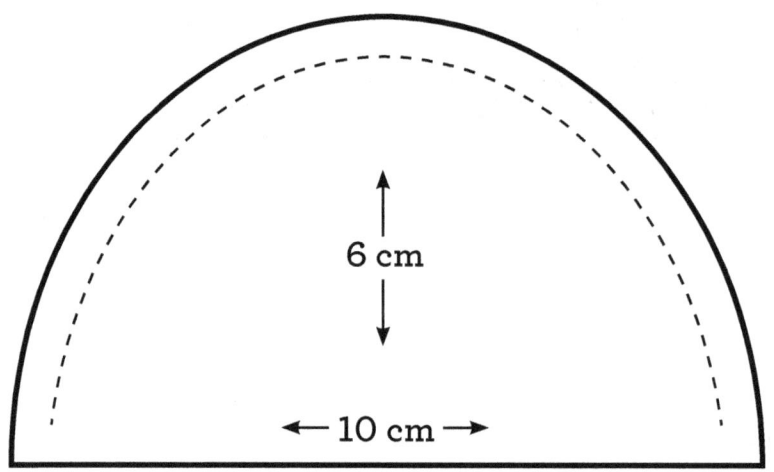

Pattern 1

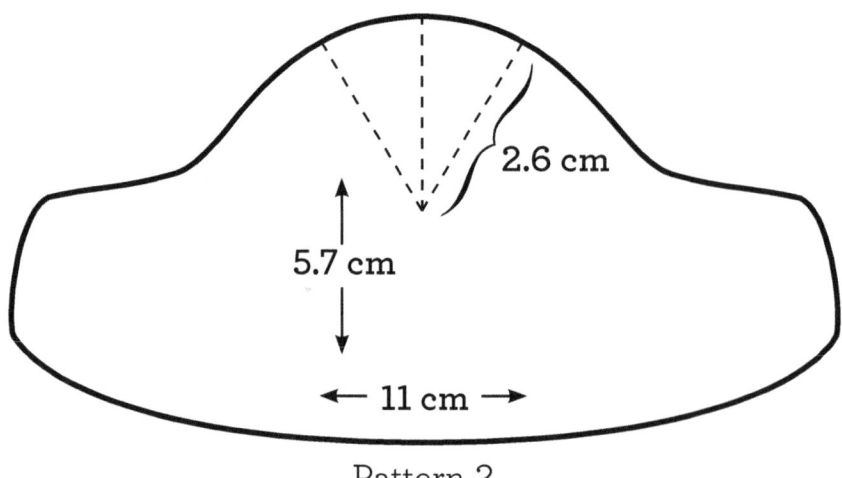

Pattern 2

Faith & Play™ | Instructions and Templates for Materials

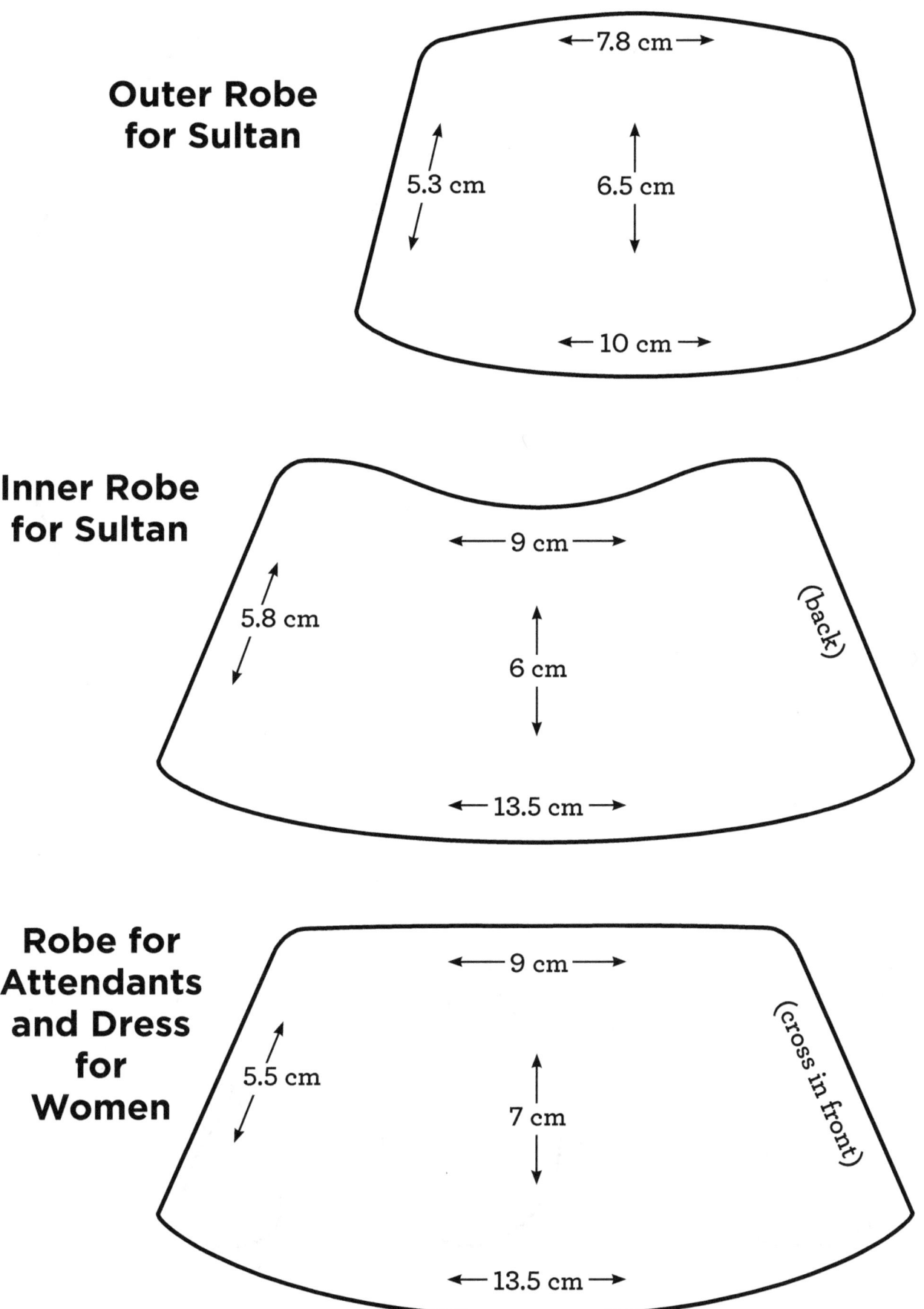

Flame Template

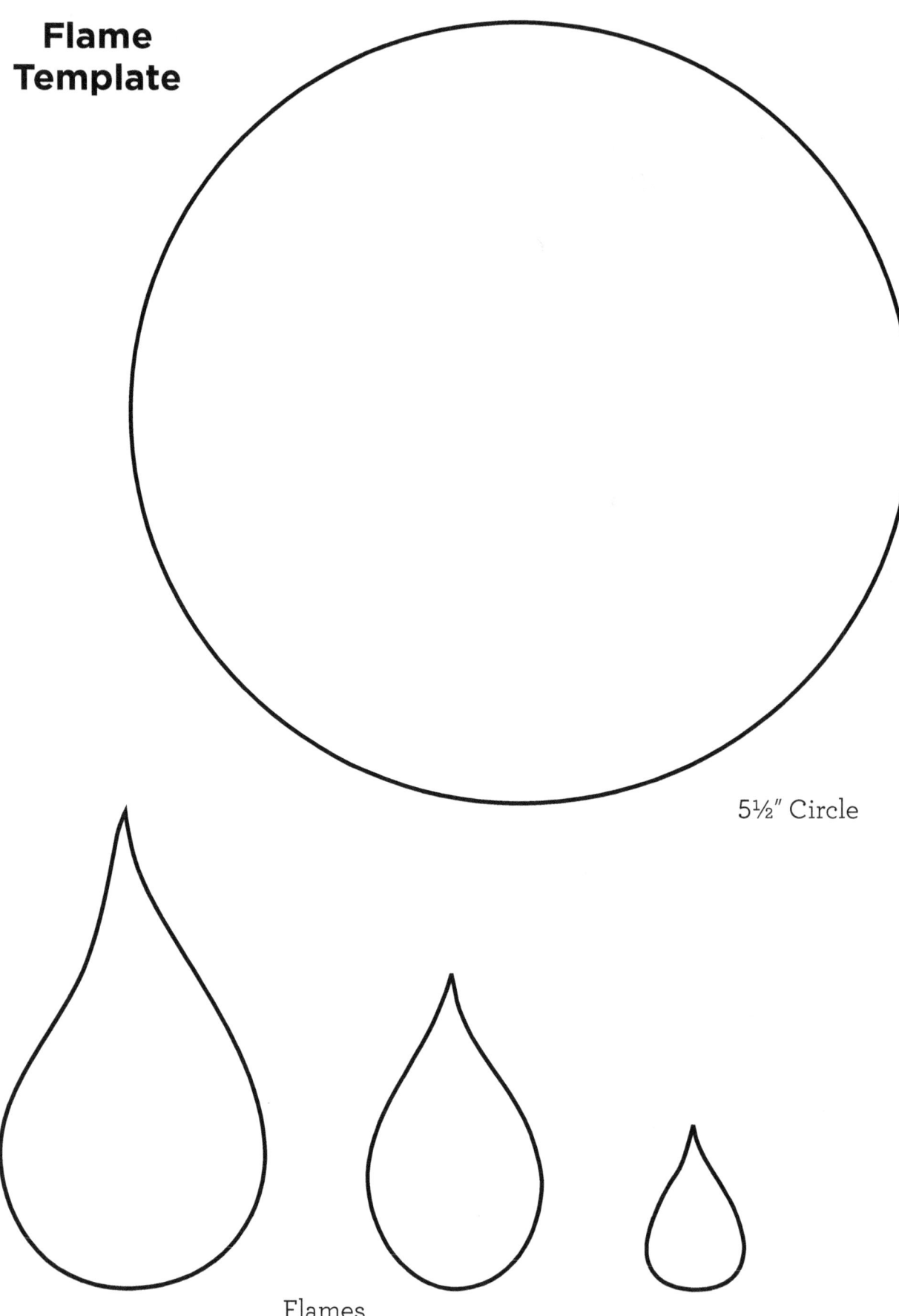

5½" Circle

Flames

132 Faith & Play™ | Instructions and Templates for Materials

www.ingramcontent.com/pod-product-compliance
Lightning Source LLC
Chambersburg PA
CBHW081229170426
43191CB00036B/2331